Mike Curry

Sara Yohe

Kirsten Rogers

Amanda Magnuson

Clare Koppel

Charlie Hall

Joey Larson

Cory Huggar

Justin Hall

Will Har

Persis Elavia

Caitlin Morris

MACMILLAN • USA

MACMILLAN
A Simon & Schuster Macmillan Company
1633 Broadway
New York, NY 10019

Library of Congress Cataloging-in-Publication Data

Crocker, Betty
 [Baking with kids]
 Betty Crocker's baking with kids
    p.   cm.
 Includes index
 ISBN: 0-02-860369-9
 1. Baking—Juvenile literature. [1. Baking.   2. Cookery.]
 TX763.C763   1995
 641.8'15—dc20   94-24258
                                                          CIP
                                                           AC

GENERAL MILLS, INC.
Betty Crocker Food and Publications Center
Director: Marcia Copeland
Editor: Karen Couné
Food Stylists: Katie W. McElroy, Cindy Syme
Nutrition Department
Nutritionist: Elyse A. Cohen, M.S.
Photographic Services
Photographer: Carolyn Luxmoore

Book design by Michele Laseau

For consistent baking results, the Betty Crocker Food and Publications Center
recommends Gold Medal flour.

Manufactured in the United States of America
10   9   8   7   6   5   4   3   2   1
First Edition
Cover: (left to right) Ice Cream Sandwiches (page 44), Strawberry Pie (page 120),
Cookies–Sour Cream Cake (page 64)

Contents

Introduction

This baking book was created just for you! You'll learn to bake delicious food, and you'll find it's fun and easy. All recipes were tested by kids to be absolutely sure they work and that they taste terrific.

Baking is very satisfying. First, you can enjoy wonderful smells from the oven, and then, you get to eat what you baked! You'll definitely want to start baking when you read these yummy recipes: Peanut Butter Cookies, Animal Cookies, The Best Brownies, Cookie-Sour Cream Cake, Top-It-Your-Way Pizza, Turtle Bread, Blueberry Streusel Muffins, Snowman Buns, Strawberry Pie, Sugar Cookie Tarts— and more! You'll also find neat ideas, like how to organize a Cookie Exchange, make your own play dough and top your toast in nifty ways.

Be sure to read "Baker's Corner" to learn everything you'll need to know when you're baking. It also explains words that may be new to you and shows the baking equipment you'll be using. And be sure an adult reads the section for them, "For the Baker's Adult Helper."

Always an ask an adult any questions you have before you start to bake. In some recipes, you'll see the words **Adult help**. It's especially important to let your adult helper know when you are baking those recipes so they will be around to help when the recipe calls for them.

Have fun with these recipes! Doing something new can be both creative and rewarding, and you can feel proud when you bake something and serve it for others to enjoy. Try making your favorite recipes, then branch out to new recipes and new taste treats. Learning to bake will give you a lifetime of good fun and good food!

Betty Crocker

Baker's Corner

Let's Get Started!

Before You Start

- Check with an adult to make sure that it's a good time to bake. Also, always let an adult know when your recipe uses the range (stove top).

- If your hair is long, tie it back so it won't get in the way.

- Wash your hands and wear an apron.

- Read the recipe all the way through before starting to cook. Ask an adult about anything you don't understand.

- Gather all the ingredients and utensils before starting to make sure that you have everything. Measure all the ingredients carefully. Put everything you need on a tray. When the tray is empty, you'll know you haven't left anything out!

- Many baked recipes use baking *soda* or baking *powder*, or some of each, as a leavening to make the recipe rise. Pay close attention when reading your recipes so that you do not get these ingredients mixed up.

- Reread the recipe to make sure that you haven't left anything out.

While You Bake

- Clean up as you bake—it makes less work at the end! As you finish using a utensil (except for sharp knives), put it in warm soapy water to soak. Wash sharp knives separately, and be careful of the sharp blades.

Finishing Up

- Wash and dry all the utensils you have used, and put them away. Wash the counters, and leave the kitchen neat and clean.

- Check the range, oven and any other appliances to be sure that you have turned them off. Put away any appliances you have used.

- Leaving the kitchen clean will make everyone glad to have you bake again. Now, enjoy your creation!

Playing It Safe in the Kitchen

Preparing the Food

- Before you use a sharp knife, can opener, blender, electric mixer or the range or oven, be sure that someone older is in the kitchen to help you and to answer questions. Watch for **Adult help:** signs throughout the recipes.

- Always dry your hands after you wash them to avoid slippery fingers.

- Wipe up any spills right away to avoid slippery floors.

- When slicing or chopping ingredients, be sure to use a cutting board.

- Always turn the sharp edge of a knife or vegetable peeler away from you and your hand when you chop or peel foods.

- Turn off the electric mixer or blender before you scrape the sides of the bowl or container so the scraper won't get caught in the blades.

- Turn off the electric mixer and make sure that it's unplugged whenever you put the beaters in or take them out.

- Put large pans on large burners, small pans on small burners. Turn the handles of pots and pans so that they don't stick out over the edge of the range, where they might accidentally be bumped, and make sure that they're not over another burner either.

When You're Baking

- If the racks need to be adjusted higher or lower, be sure to arrange them before you turn on the oven.

- Allow plenty of air space around foods you're baking—no pans or dishes should touch.

- Arrange foods on oven racks so that one isn't placed directly over another.

- Use a tight-fitting lid or aluminum foil when the recipe calls for covering. Uncover cooked foods away from you, and keep your face away from the steam.

- Always use thick, dry pot holders to avoid burns, not thin or wet ones.

- Ask an adult to help you put pans into and take pans out of the oven.

- Ask an adult to help when checking if a recipe is done. Close the oven door quickly when you have finished looking in, so that heat won't be lost.

- Be careful where you put hot pans. Only put them on a surface that is dry and can withstand heat.

For the Baker's Adult Helper

Preparing food for themselves and others is a very satisfying endeavor for children, and children love to bake! There are precautions that must be taught. Your supervision along with some simple rules can make it fun and, more importantly, safe for boys and girls to fix their own snacks and help prepare meals. You are the best judge of the age at which a child should be allowed to use the range, oven, other appliances or sharp knives. Follow these simple steps to help children cook safely:

- Read the recipe all the way through with the child before they start to cook. Explain anything they don't understand.

- We recommend adult supervision whenever children use sharp knives, the range, the oven or small appliances.

- Children should be taught how to correctly set the controls on the range and oven.

- Provide pot holders in a size that's easy for smaller, less adept hands to use.

- Teach children safe food-preparation techniques and how to handle hot foods.

Kitchen Computing

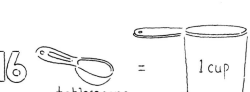

Baker's Talk

Beat: Make smooth with a vigorous stirring motion using a spoon, wire whisk, egg-beater or electric mixer.

Boil: Heat liquid until bubbles keep rising and breaking on the surface.

Chop: Cut food into small, uneven pieces; a sharp knife, food chopper or food processor may be used.

Core: Cut out the stem end and remove the seeds.

Cut in: Mix fat into a flour mixture with a pastry blender using a rolling motion or by cutting with a fork or two knives until particles are size specified.

Dice: Cut into cubes smaller than 1/2 inch.

Drain: Pour off liquid or let it run off through the holes in a strainer or colander, as when draining cooked pasta or ground beef. Or, remove pieces of food from a fat or liquid and set them on paper towels to soak up excess moisture.

Flute: Flatten pastry evenly on rim of pie plate and press firmly around rim with tines of fork.

Grate: Rub against grater to cut into small pieces.

Grease: Spread the bottom and sides of a dish with butter or shortening using a pastry brush or paper towel.

Knead: Curve your fingers and fold dough toward you, then push it away with the heels of your hands, using a quick, rocking motion.

Mix: Combine to distribute ingredients evenly using a spoon, fork, blender or an electric mixer.

Peel: Cut off the skin with a knife or peel with fingers.

Pipe: Press out frosting from a decorating bag using steady pressure to form a design or write a message. To finish a design, stop the pressure and lift the point up and away.

Roll or pat: Flatten and spread with a floured rolling pin or hands.

Utensils You Should Have

For Preparation

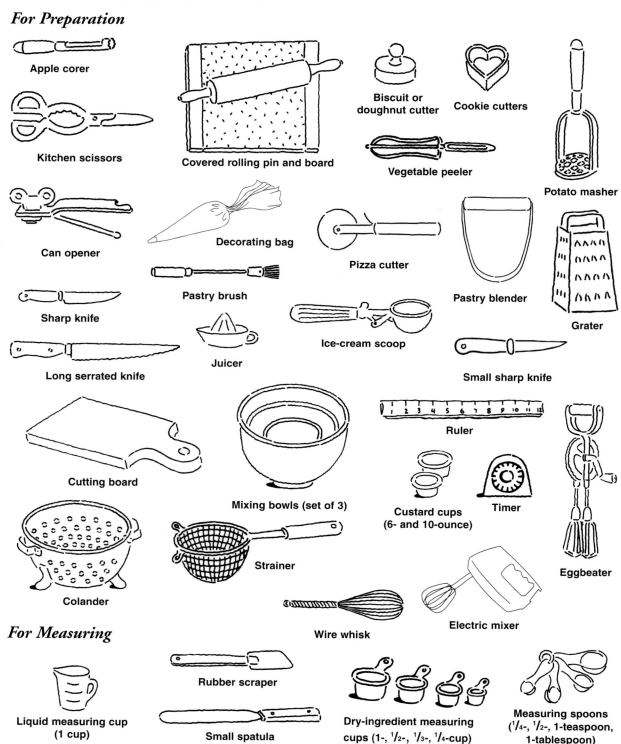

Apple corer

Kitchen scissors

Covered rolling pin and board

Biscuit or doughnut cutter

Cookie cutters

Vegetable peeler

Potato masher

Can opener

Decorating bag

Pizza cutter

Pastry blender

Pastry brush

Grater

Sharp knife

Ice-cream scoop

Juicer

Long serrated knife

Small sharp knife

Cutting board

Mixing bowls (set of 3)

Ruler

Custard cups
(6- and 10-ounce)

Timer

Eggbeater

Colander

Strainer

Wire whisk

Electric mixer

For Measuring

Rubber scraper

Liquid measuring cup
(1 cup)

Small spatula

Dry-ingredient measuring
cups (1-, 1/2-, 1/3-, 1/4-cup)

Measuring spoons
(1/4-, 1/2-, 1-teaspoon,
1-tablespoon)

For Top-of-Range Cooking

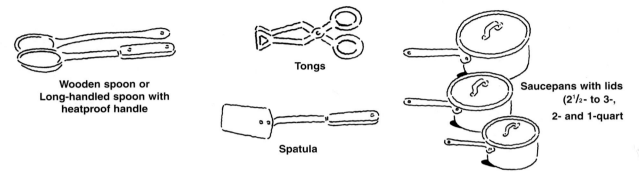

Wooden spoon or Long-handled spoon with heatproof handle

Tongs

Spatula

Saucepans with lids (2$^1\!/_2$- to 3-, 2- and 1-quart

For Baking

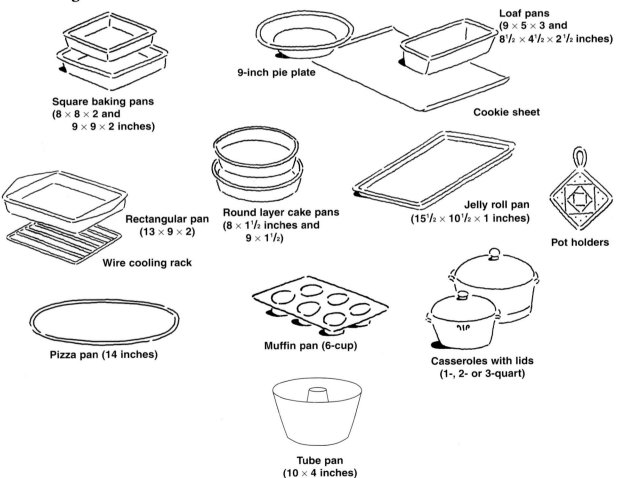

Square baking pans (8 × 8 × 2 and 9 × 9 × 2 inches)

9-inch pie plate

Loaf pans (9 × 5 × 3 and 8$^1\!/_2$ × 4$^1\!/_2$ × 2$^1\!/_2$ inches)

Cookie sheet

Rectangular pan (13 × 9 × 2)

Wire cooling rack

Round layer cake pans (8 × 1$^1\!/_2$ inches and 9 × 1$^1\!/_2$)

Jelly roll pan (15$^1\!/_2$ × 10$^1\!/_2$ × 1 inches)

Pot holders

Pizza pan (14 inches)

Muffin pan (6-cup)

Casseroles with lids (1-, 2- or 3-quart)

Tube pan (10 × 4 inches)

Measuring Up

All-purpose Flour. Spoon flour lightly into dry-ingredient measuring cup. Level with spatula. Bisquick® baking mix and granulated and powdered sugars are measured the same way.

Baking Powder. Dip and fill measuring spoon. Level with spatula. Baking soda, cream of tartar and spices are measured in the same way. Liquids, like vanilla, can also be measured in measuring spoons.

Chopped Nuts. Pack lightly into dry-ingredient measuring cup. Also measure shredded cheese, soft bread crumbs and shredded coconut this way.

Brown Sugar. Pack firmly into dry-ingredient measuring cup. Level with spatula.

Shortening. Pack firmly into dry-ingredient measuring cup. Level with spatula and remove with rubber scraper.

Molasses and Corn Syrup. Pour into liquid measuring cup. Remove with rubber scraper.

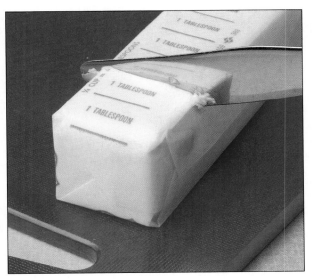

Margarine or Butter. Cut using measurement marks on the wrapper as a guide.

Milk and Other Liquids. Set liquid measuring cup on counter. Pour in the liquid. Bend down to check the correct amount at eye level.

1

▲▲▲▲▲▲

Crazy About Cookies, Brownies and Bars

Animal Cookies (page 36)

▲▲▲▲ "GINGERPOP" COOKIES ▲▲▲▲

About 18 cookies

🍴🥄 Utensils You Will Need

Large bowl • Liquid measuring cup • Wooden spoons • Plastic wrap •
18 flat wooden ice-cream sticks • Cookie sheet • Glass • Pot holders • Spatula •
Wire cooling rack • Small bowl • Knife

1 Mix in large bowl with wooden spoon ► **1 package (14.5 ounces) gingerbread cake and cookie mix**
1/3 cup lukewarm water

2 Cover dough with plastic wrap and refrigerate about 15 minutes or until slightly firm.

3 Heat oven to 375°.

4 Shape dough into 18 1 1/4-inch balls. Poke 1 ice-cream stick into the side of each ball until tip of stick is in center of ball. Put balls about 2 inches apart on cookie sheet.

5 Flatten balls gently with bottom of glass dipped in ► **Sugar**

6 Bake 8 to 10 minutes or until edges are firm. Cool cookies on cookie sheet 1 minute, then remove with spatula to wire rack. Cool completely.

7 Mix in small bowl with wooden spoon ► **1 cup vanilla ready-to-spread frosting**
2 drops red food color

8 Spread frosting over each cookie with knife, then immediately make face or decorate as you like with ► **Assorted candies (candy-coated chocolate candies, candy corn, licorice or gumdrops)**

Nutrition Per Cookie: Calories 155 (Calories from Fat 45); Fat 5g (Saturated 1); Cholesterol 0mg; Sodium 1mg; Carbohydrate 27g (Dietary Fiber 0g); Protein 1g

Although Amanda thought the dough was kind of hard to roll into balls, she also thought it was fun to make and decorate the cookies. And, she said, everyone liked them! We want to assure Amanda that, just like most things, shaping cookie dough does get easier with practice.

HINT
If dough is too soft to shape into balls, cover with plastic wrap and refrigerate about 1 hour. When flattening balls of dough with a glass, you may want to lightly grease the bottom of the glass with shortening to help the sugar stick to the glass.

HOLIDAY HONEY COOKIES

About 42 cookies *(photo page 22)*

Utensils You Will Need

Cookie sheet • Pastry brush • Large bowl • Dry-ingredient measuring cups •
Small sharp knife • Measuring spoons • Wooden spoon • Rolling pin • Ruler •
2-inch cookie cutters • Pot holders • Spatula • Wire cooling rack

1 Heat oven to 375°.

2 Lightly grease cookie sheet with – – ➤ | **Shortening** |

3 Mix in large bowl with wooden
spoon – – – – – – – – – ➤

| **1/3 cup powdered sugar** |
| **1/3 cup margarine or butter,** |
| **softened** |
| **2/3 cup honey** |
| **1 teaspoon almond extract** |
| **1 large egg** |

4 Stir in – – – – – – – – – ➤

| **2 3/4 cups all-purpose flour** |
| **1 teaspoon baking soda** |
| **1/2 teaspoon salt** |

5 Sprinkle a clean surface (such as a
kitchen counter or breadboard) with
flour. Put dough on surface. Roll
dough until 1/8 inch thick. Cut with cookie cutters. Put cookies about
1 inch apart on cookie sheet.

6 Bake 6 to 8 minutes or until light brown. Watch carefully because cookies
brown quickly. Immediately remove cookies from cookie sheet with spatula
to wire rack. Cool completely.

7 Frost cookies with – – – – – – ➤ | **Glaze (right)** |

8 Decorate cookies with – – – – ➤ | **Decorator's Frosting (right)** |

GLAZE Medium bowl • Dry-ingredient measuring cup • Measuring spoons • Wooden spoon

1 Mix in medium bowl with wooden spoon until smooth - - - - - - →

> **2 cups powdered sugar**
> **1/4 teaspoon almond extract**
> **2 tablespoons water**

2 Stir in, 1 teaspoon at a time, until spreadable - - - - - - - →

> **2 to 4 teaspoons water**

DECORATOR'S FROSTING Small bowl • Dry-ingredient measuring cup • Measuring spoons • Wooden spoon

1 Mix in small bowl with wooden spoon, adding the water 1 teaspoon at a time, until frosting is thin enough to drizzle or thick enough to be used in a decorating bag - - - - - - - - →

> **1 cup powdered sugar**
> **3 or 4 drops food color**
> **3 to 5 teaspoons water**

Nutrition Per Cookie: Calories 100 (Calories from Fat 20); Fat 2g (Saturated 0g); Cholesterol 5mg; Sodium 75mg; Carbohydrate 20g (Dietary Fiber 0g); Protein 1g

When we asked Clare to test these cookies, we called them Hanukkah Honey Cookies. While making them, she thought they would be great cut out in any holiday shapes and suggested that we change their name to Holiday Honey Cookies, which we did! Good idea, Clare!

HINT
If dough is too soft to roll, cover with plastic wrap and refrigerate about 2 hours.

▲▲▲▲ EASY SUGAR COOKIES ▲▲▲▲

About 48 cookies

Utensils You Will Need

Large bowl • Dry-ingredient measuring cups • Measuring spoons •
Wooden spoon • Cookie sheet • Teaspoon • Glass • Pot holders •
Spatula • Wire cooling rack • Small bowl

1 Heat oven to 375°.

2 Beat in large bowl with wooden spoon until smooth ‑ ‑ ‑ ‑ ‑ ‑ ►

> **1 cup sugar**
> **1 cup (2 sticks) margarine or butter, softened**
> **1/2 teaspoon vanilla**
> **1 large egg**

3 Stir in ‑ ‑ ‑ ‑ ‑ ‑ ‑ ‑ ►

> **2 1/4 cups all-purpose flour**

4 Shape dough by teaspoonfuls into balls. Put balls about 2 inches apart on cookie sheet.

5 Flatten balls gently with bottom of glass dipped in ‑ ‑ ‑ ‑ ‑ ‑ ►

> **Sugar, colored sugar or candy sprinkles**

6 Bake 10 to 12 minutes or until set and edges just begin to brown. Cool cookies on cookie sheet 1 minute, then remove with spatula to wire rack. Cool.

Nutrition Per Cookie: Calories 75 (Calories from Fat 35); Fat 4g (Saturated 1); Cholesterol 5mg; Sodium 45mg; Carbohydrate 9g (Dietary Fiber 0g); Protein 1g

HINT
If dough is too soft to shape, cover with plastic wrap and refrigerate about 1 hour.

Holiday Honey Cookies (page 20)

▲▲▲▲▲ SANTA CLAUS COOKIES ▲▲▲▲▲

About 30 cookies

Utensils You Will Need

Large bowl • Dry-ingredient measuring cups • Measuring spoons • Wooden spoons • Ruler • Cookie sheet • Glass • Pot holders • Spatula • Wire cooling rack • Small bowl • Knife

1 Heat oven to 400°.

2 Mix in large bowl with wooden spoon ---------→

> 1 cup granulated sugar
> 1/2 cup shortening
> 2 tablespoons milk
> 1 large egg

3 Stir in ---------→

> 2 cups all-purpose flour
> 1 teaspoon baking powder
> 1/2 teaspoon baking soda
> 1/2 teaspoon salt

4 Shape dough into 1 1/4-inch balls. Put balls about 2 inches apart on cookie sheet.

5 Flatten balls until about 2 1/2 inches across with bottom of glass dipped in ---------→

> Sugar

6 Bake 8 to 10 minutes or until edges are light brown. Immediately remove cookies from cookie sheet with spatula to wire rack. Cool completely.

7 For frosting, mix in small bowl with wooden spoon, adding the water 1 teaspoon at a time, until spreadable ---------→

> 1 1/2 cups powdered sugar
> 1/2 teaspoon vanilla
> 2 to 3 tablespoons water

8 To decorate cookies, you will need about ▬ ▬ ▬ ▬ ▬ ▬ ▬ ▬ ▬ ▬ ▬ ▬ ▬ ▬ ➤

> **3 tablespoons red sugar**
> **1/2 cup shredded coconut**
> **30 miniature marshmallows**
> **60 currants or raisins**
> **30 red cinnamon candies**

9 Spread frosting on 1 cookie at a time, then sprinkle red sugar on top third of cookie for hat and sprinkle coconut on bottom third for beard. Press on 1 marshmallow for tassel of hat, 2 currants for eyes and 1 cinnamon candy for nose.

Here's another idea. . . Make **Santa Claus Cookie Pops:** Before baking, poke 1 flat wooden ice-cream stick into the side of each flattened ball of dough until tip of stick is in center of ball.

Nutrition Per Cookie: Calories 135 (Calories from Fat 35); Fat 4g (Saturated 1g); Cholesterol 10mg; Sodium 80mg; Carbohydrate 24g (Dietary Fiber 0g); Protein 1g

GIANT COLORFUL
▲▲▲▲▲ CANDY COOKIES ▲▲▲▲▲

About 18 cookies

Utensils You Will Need

Large bowl • Dry-ingredient measuring cups • Electric mixer • Measuring spoons • Wooden spoon • Cookie sheet • Ruler • Fork • Pot holders • Spatula • Wire cooling rack

1 Heat oven to 375°.

2 Beat in large bowl with electric mixer on medium speed about 5 minutes or until fluffy ▸

> **1 cup packed brown sugar**
> **3/4 cup granulated sugar**
> **1 cup (2 sticks) margarine or butter, softened**

3 Beat in ▸

> **1 teaspoon vanilla**
> **2 large eggs**
> **2 1/2 cups all-purpose flour**
> **3/4 teaspoon salt**
> **3/4 teaspoon baking soda**

4 Stir in ▸

> **2 cups candy-coated chocolate candies**

5 Drop dough by 1/4 cupfuls about 2 inches apart onto cookie sheet. Flatten dough gently with fork.

6 Bake 11 to 14 minutes or until edges are light brown. Cool cookies 3 to 4 minutes on cookie sheet, then carefully remove with spatula to wire rack. Cool.

Here's another idea. . . . Make **Giant Chocolate Chip Cookies:** Leave out candy-coated chocolate candies. Stir in 2 cups semisweet chocolate chips instead.

Nutrition Per Cookie: Calories 355 (Calories from Fat 145); Fat 16g (Saturated 5g); Cholesterol 25mg; Sodium 300mg; Carbohydrate 50g (Dietary Fiber 1g); Protein 4g

While testing these cookies, Charlie learned that you should always pack brown sugar when measuring it. His mom showed him how to press it down with the back of a spoon as he put each scoop into the cup.

▲▲▲▲▲ SLICE 'N EASY COOKIES ▲▲▲▲▲

About 66 cookies

Utensils You Will Need

Large bowl • Dry-ingredient measuring cups • Small sharp knife • Measuring spoons • Wooden spoon • Plastic wrap • Ruler • Sharp knife • Cookie sheet • Pot holders • Spatula • Wire cooling rack

1 Mix in large bowl with wooden spoon ⇒

> **1 cup granulated sugar**
> **1 cup packed brown sugar**
> **2/3 cup shortening**
> **2/3 cup margarine or butter, softened**
> **2 teaspoons vanilla**
> **2 large eggs**

2 Stir in ⇒

> **3 1/4 cups all-purpose flour**
> **1/2 cup cocoa**
> **1 teaspoon baking soda**
> **1 teaspoon salt**

3 Sprinkle a clean surface (such as a kitchen counter or breadboard) with flour. Put dough on surface. Shape dough into a ball with lightly floured hands, pressing to pack tightly. Cut dough in half. Shape each half into a roll, about 2 inches across and about 8 inches long, by gently rolling dough back and forth on floured surface. Roll dough onto plastic wrap. Wrap plastic wrap around dough and twist ends tightly.

4 Refrigerate rolls at least 8 hours. (Rolls can be refrigerated up to 1 month or frozen up to 3 months.)

5 Heat oven to 375°.

6 Unwrap rolls. **Adult help:** Cut rolls into 1/4-inch slices. (It is not necessary to thaw frozen rolls before slicing.) Put slices about 2 inches apart on cookie sheet.

7 Bake 6 to 8 minutes or until set. Immediately remove cookies from cookie sheet with spatula to wire rack. Cool.

Here's another idea. . . Make **Chocolate Chip Cookies:** Leave out cocoa. Stir in 1 cup miniature semisweet chocolate chips and 1 cup chopped nuts with the flour.

Here's another idea. . . Make **Mint Sandwich Cookies:** Cut refrigerated or frozen rolls into 1/8-inch slices. Bake about 6 minutes or until set. For filling, mix 4 cups powdered sugar, 1/2 cup (1 stick) margarine or butter, softened, and 1 teaspoon mint extract. Stir in 3 to 4 tablespoons water, 1 teaspoon at a time, until smooth and spreadable. Stir in a few drops of green or red food color to tint frosting, if you like. Put cooled cookies together in pairs with mint filling.

Nutrition Per Cookie: Calories 90 (Calories from Fat 35); Fat 4g (Saturated 1g); Cholesterol 5mg; Sodium 80mg; Carbohydrate 12g (Dietary Fiber 0g); Protein 1g

Caitlin has big plans for these easy cookies. She suggests turning them into a super dessert by serving them with a scoop of vanilla ice cream and chocolate sauce on top.

▲▲▲▲▲ ROCKY ROAD COOKIES ▲▲▲▲▲

About 48 cookies

Utensils You Will Need

1-quart saucepan • Dry-ingredient measuring cups • Wooden spoons •
Small sharp knife • Large bowl • Measuring spoons • Teaspoon • Cookie sheet
• Ruler • Pot holders • Spatula • Wire cooling rack

1 Melt in saucepan over low heat, stirring a few times, then remove from heat and cool slightly ‑ ‑ ‑ ‑ ‑ ‑ ➤

> **1/2 cup semisweet chocolate chips**
> **1/2 cup (1 stick) margarine or butter**

2 Heat oven to 400°.

3 Mix in large bowl with wooden spoon ‑ ‑ ‑ ‑ ‑ ‑ ➤

> **1 1/2 cups all-purpose flour**
> **1 cup sugar**
> **1/2 teaspoon baking powder**
> **1/2 teaspoon vanilla**
> **1/4 teaspoon salt**
> **2 large eggs**
> **1 cup chopped nuts**
> **1/2 cup semisweet chocolate chips**
> **The melted chocolate mixture**

4 Drop dough by rounded teaspoonfuls about 2 inches apart onto cookie sheet.

5 Press into center of each cookie 1 of ‑ ‑ ‑ ‑ ‑ ‑ ➤

> **About 48 miniature marshmallows**

6 Bake 8 to 12 minutes or until almost no mark stays when cookie is touched. Immediately remove cookies from cookie sheet with spatula to wire rack. Cool.

Nutrition Per Cookie: Calories 95 (Calories from Fat 45); Fat 5g (Saturated 1g); Cholesterol 10mg; Sodium 45mg; Carbohydrate 11g (Dietary Fiber 0g); Protein 1g

Joey thought these cookies were fun to make and especially liked cracking the eggs and pressing the marshmallows into the middle of each cookie.

▲▲▲▲▲ PEANUT BUTTER COOKIES ▲▲▲▲

About 36 cookies

Utensils You Will Need

Large bowl • Dry-ingredient measuring cups • Small sharp knife • Wooden spoon • Measuring spoons • Plastic wrap • Ruler • Cookie sheet • Fork • Pot holders • Spatula • Wire cooling rack

1 Heat oven to 375°.

2 Mix in large bowl with wooden spoon ▬ ▬ ▬ ▬ ▬ ▬ ▬ ➤

> 1/2 cup granulated sugar
> 1/2 cup packed brown sugar
> 1/2 cup peanut butter
> 1/4 cup shortening
> 1/4 cup (1/2 stick) margarine
> or butter, softened
> 1 large egg

3 Stir in ▬ ▬ ▬ ▬ ▬ ▬ ▬ ▬ ➤

> 1 1/4 cups all-purpose or whole wheat flour
> 3/4 teaspoon baking soda
> 1/2 teaspoon baking powder
> 1/4 teaspoon salt

4 Shape dough into 1 1/4-inch balls. Put balls about 3 inches apart on cookie sheet. Flatten balls gently in crisscross pattern with fork dipped in sugar.

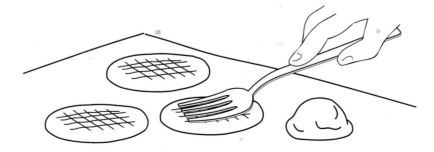

5 Bake 9 to 10 minutes or until light brown. Cool cookies 2 minutes on cookie sheet, then remove with spatula to wire rack. Cool.

Here's another idea. . . Make **Quick Peanut Butter Sticks**: Divide dough into fourths. Shape fourths into strips, 10 inches long by 1 1/2 inches wide, on cookie sheets. (Two strips can fit on 1 cookie sheet.) Flatten strips to 3 inches wide with fork dipped in sugar. Bake 10 to 12 minutes or until golden brown. Cool 2 minutes, then cut each strip cross- wise into 1-inch slices. Remove cookies from cookie sheet with spatula to wire rack. Cool. About 42 cookies.

HINT
If dough is too soft to shape into balls, cover with plastic wrap and refrigerate about 1 hour.

Nutrition Per Cookie: Calories 90 (Calories from Fat 45); Fat 5g (Saturated 1g); Cholesterol 5mg; Sodium 85mg; Carbohydrate 10g (Dietary Fiber 0g); Protein 1g

▲▲▲▲▲ CARAMEL-NUT COOKIES ▲▲▲▲▲

About 32 cookies

Utensils You Will Need

Large bowl • Dry-ingredient measuring cups • Measuring spoons • Wooden spoons • Cookie sheet • Sharp knife • Cutting board • Teaspoon • Pot holders • Spatula • Wire cooling rack • l-quart saucepan • Knife

1 Mix in large bowl with wooden spoon – – – – – – – →

> **1/2 cup packed brown sugar**
> **1/2 (1 stick) margarine or butter, softened**
> **2 tablespoons water**
> **1 teaspoon vanilla**

2 Stir in until dough holds together (if dough is dry, stir in 1 to 2 teaspoons water) – – – – – →

> **1 1/2 cups all-purpose flour**
> **1/8 teaspoon salt**

3 Heat oven to 350°.

4 To assemble cookies, you will need about – – – – – – – – – →

> **160 pecan halves (about 2 1/4 cups)**
> **8 vanilla caramels, unwrapped**

5 **Adult help:** Cut each caramel into 4 pieces with sharp knife.

6 For each cookie, group 5 pecan halves on cookie sheet (for legs and head of turtle). Shape 1 teaspoon dough around each caramel piece to form a ball. Press ball firmly onto center of each turtle.

7 Bake 12 to 15 minutes or until set but not brown. Immediately remove cookies from cookie sheet with spatula to wire rack. Cool completely.

8 Melt in saucepan over low heat, stirring a few times, then remove from heat ━ ━ ━ ━ ━ ━ ━ ━ ➤

1 ounce unsweetened chocolate

9 Beat into chocolate with wooden spoon, adding the water 1 teaspoon at a time, until smooth ━ ━ ━ ━ ━ ━ ➤

1 cup powdered sugar
1 teaspoon vanilla
2 to 4 teaspoons water

10 Spread tops of cookies with chocolate glaze.

Nutrition Per Cookie: *Calories 115 (Calories from Fat 55); Fat 6g (Saturated 1g); Cholesterol 0mg; Sodium 50mg; Carbohydrate 14g (Dietary Fiber 0g); Protein 1g*

▲▲▲▲▲ ANIMAL COOKIES ▲▲▲▲▲

About 30 cookies *(photo page 17)*

Utensils You Will Need

Large bowl • Dry-ingredient measuring cups • Measuring spoons •
Wooden spoon • Plastic wrap • Tablespoon • Cookie sheet • Pot holders •
Spatula • Wire cooling rack

1 Heat oven to 350°.

2 Mix in large bowl with wooden
spoon ► ► ► ►

> 1/2 cup granulated sugar
> 1/2 cup packed brown sugar
> 1/2 cup (1 stick) margarine or
> butter, softened
> 1 teaspoon vanilla
> 1 large egg

3 Stir in ► ► ► ►

> 2 cups all-purpose flour
> 1 teaspoon baking powder
> 1/2 teaspoon salt
> 1/2 teaspoon ground cinnamon

4 Shape dough by 2 tablespoonfuls into
slightly flattened balls and ropes. Make
animal shapes with balls and ropes of
dough on cookie sheet.

5 Bake 10 to 12 minutes or until edges are golden brown. Cool cookies 3
minutes on cookie sheet, then remove with spatula to wire rack. Cool.

Here's another idea. . . Make **Letter and Number Cookies**: Make dough as directed. Shape dough by level tablespoonfuls into ropes, about 8 inches long and about 1/4 inch thick. Shape into letters and numbers as desired on cookie sheet. Bake 8 to 10 minutes. About 3 dozen cookies.

Nutrition Per Cookie: Calories 85 (Calories from Fat 25); Fat 3g (Saturated 1g); Cholesterol 10mg; Sodium 90mg; Carbohydrate 13g (Dietary Fiber 0g); Protein 1g

HINT

If dough is too soft to shape, cover with plastic wrap and refrigerate about 2 hours or until firm.

KIDS' HOLIDAY COOKIE EXCHANGE

What could be better than having a holiday party and being with your friends and then when the party is over, you have a bunch of different cookies? That's what a cookie exchange is all about—friends sharing good times and good cookies!

To plan a cookie exchange:

1 Plan the date and time with your parents or an adult who will supervise the event. Decide if you want to send recipes to your friends for them to make or take pot-luck on whatever they want to make.

2 Plan for treats and activities that are appropriate for the weather in your part of the country. If you live where there will be snow, arrange to go sledding or ice skating. If you live in a warmer area, plan to go roller skating or hiking. Indoor activities and games would also be fun. Hot chocolate and Gingerbread Muffins with Orange Spread (page 104) would be a great snack for afterwards.

3 Send invitations to about 5 friends and ask them each to bring a recipe of cookies to the party. You can invite more or fewer kids, depending on your wishes.

4 When it's time to share the cookies, put them all out around a table. Divide each batch of cookies by the number of kids who are at the party. Provide boxes and containers or paper plates and plastic bags and let everyone go around the table and pack up the correct number of cookies to take home.

Cookie Ideas for a Cookie Exchange

Easy Sugar Cookies (page 23)

Santa Claus Cookies (page 24)

Slice 'n Easy Cookies (Chocolate Chip Variation) (page 28)

Caramel-Nut Cookies (page 34)

Double Mint Brownies (page 48)

Peanut Butter and Jam Bars (page 50)

Cookie Exchange—Easy Sugar Cookies (page 23), Santa Claus Cookies (page 24),
Slice 'n Easy Cookies (page 28), Peanut Butter and Jam Bars (page 50)

▲▲▲▲▲ BUMBLEBEES ▲▲▲▲▲

About 48 cookies

🍴 Utensils You Will Need

Large bowl • Dry-ingredient measuring cups • Liquid measuring cup •
Wooden spoon • Measuring spoons • Plastic wrap • Ruler • Cookie sheet •
Pot holders • Spatula • Wire cooling rack

1 Mix in large bowl with wooden
spoon - - - - - - - - - ➤

> **1/2 cup peanut butter**
> **1/2 cup shortening**
> **1/3 cup packed brown sugar**
> **1/3 cup honey**
> **1 large egg**

2 Stir in - - - - - - - - - ➤

> **1 3/4 cups all-purpose flour**
> **3/4 teaspoon baking soda**
> **1/2 teaspoon baking powder**

3 Cover dough with plastic wrap and
refrigerate about 2 hours or until firm.

4 Heat oven to 350°.

5 Shape dough into 1-inch balls. (Dough will be slightly sticky.)

6 To assemble cookies, you will need
about - - - - - - - - - ➤

> **8 dozen pretzel twists**
> **8 dozen pretzel sticks**

7 For each cookie, put 2 pretzel twists
side by side on cookie sheet, with
rounded sides touching. Put 1 ball of dough in center, and flatten gently.

8 Break 2 pretzel sticks in half. Gently press 3 pretzel stick halves into dough
for stripes on bee. Break last pretzel piece in half. Poke pieces in 1 end of
dough for antennae.

9 Bake 11 to 13 minutes or until light golden brown. Immediately remove
cookies from cookie sheet with spatula to wire rack. Cool.

Nutrition Per Cookie: *Calories 85 (Calories from Fat 35); Fat 4g (Saturated 1g); Cholesterol 5mg;
Sodium 120mg; Carbohydrate 11g (Dietary Fiber 0g); Protein 1g*

Bumblebees, Super Snack Bars (page 49)

▲▲▲▲▲ MULTIGRAIN CUTOUTS ▲▲▲▲▲

About 70 cookies

Utensils You Will Need

Large bowl • Dry-ingredient measuring cups • Liquid measuring cups •
Measuring spoons • Wooden spoon • Rolling pin • Ruler • Cookie cutters •
Cookie sheet • Decorating bag • Pot holders • Spatula • Wire cooling rack

1 Heat oven to 350°.

2 Mix in large bowl with wooden spoon ■ ■ ■ ■ ■ ■ ■ ■ ➤

> **1 cup sugar**
> **2/3 cup shortening**
> **3 1/4 cups whole wheat flour**
> **1/4 cup cornmeal**
> **1/4 cup wheat germ**
> **3/4 cup milk**
> **1 teaspoon baking powder**
> **1/2 teaspoon salt**
> **1/2 teaspoon vanilla**

3 Sprinkle a clean surface (such as a kitchen counter or breadboard) with flour. Put dough on surface. Divide dough into 3 parts. Roll 1 part of dough at a time until 1/8 inch thick. Cut dough with cookie cutters. Put cookies on cookie sheet.

4 Put in decorating bag with #5 writing tip and outline or decorate unbaked cookies with ■ ■ ➤

> **Baked-on Frosting (right)**

5 Bake 12 to 14 minutes or until edges are light brown. Cool 1 minute on cookie sheet, then remove with spatula to wire rack. Cool.

BAKED-ON FROSTING Small bowl • Dry-ingredient
measuring cup • Small sharp knife • Wooden spoon • Measuring spoon

1 Mix in small bowl with wooden
spoon until smooth ▶

> **2/3 cup all-purpose flour**
> **2/3 cup margarine or butter,**
> **softened**

2 Stir in, 1 teaspoon at a time, until
spreadable ▶

> **3 to 4 teaspoons hot water**

*Nutrition Per Cookie: Calories 70 (Calories from
Fat 35); Fat 4g (Saturated 1g); Cholesterol 0mg;
Sodium 45mg; Carbohydrate 9g (Dietary Fiber 1g); Protein 1g*

HINT
*If you don't have a decorating bag,
you can make one with a plastic bag
or paper envelope. Put frosting in the
corner of a plastic bag and seal, or put
frosting in the corner of an envelope and
fold the other end over. Snip a small piece
off the corner of the bag or envelope to
make a writing tip.*

**Will had fun making and eating this healthy
snack. His younger brothers and sister helped cut
out some of the shapes.**

ICE-CREAM SANDWICHES

About 18 sandwich cookies

Utensils You Will Need

Tablespoon • Dry-ingredient measuring cup • Measuring spoon • Rectangular pan, 13 × 9 × 2 inches • 1-quart saucepan • Wooden spoon • Plastic wrap

1 Make and let cool - - - - - → **Peanut Butter Cookies (page 32)**

2 To assemble ice-cream sandwiches, you will need about - - - - - → **2 cups ice cream (any flavor), slightly softened**

3 For each ice-cream sandwich, press 1 rounded tablespoon ice cream between 2 cookies. Put sandwiches in rectangular pan and freeze uncovered about 1 hour until firm.

4 If you like, roll the edges of the sandwiches in - - - - - → **Candies or chopped dry-roasted peanuts**

5 Wrap each sandwich in plastic wrap. Store sandwiches in freezer in plastic freezer bag.

Nutrition Per Sandwich: Calories 205 (Calories from Fat 100); Fat 11g (Saturated 3g); Cholesterol 20mg; Sodium 180mg; Carbohydrate 23g (Dietary Fiber 1g); Protein 4g

Peanut Butter Cookies (page 32), Ice-cream Sandwiches

▲▲▲▲ THE BEST BROWNIES ▲▲▲▲

24 brownies

Utensils You Will Need

Square pan, 9 × 9 × 2 inches • Pastry brush • l-quart saucepan • Small sharp knife • Wooden spoons • Large bowl • Dry-ingredient measuring cups • Measuring spoons • Electric mixer • Pot holders • Wire cooling rack • Ruler

1 Heat oven to 350°.

2 Grease square pan with ➤ **Shortening**

3 Melt in saucepan over low heat, stirring a few times, then remove from heat and cool slightly ➤ **5 ounces unsweetened chocolate / 2/3 cup margarine or butter**

4 Beat in large bowl with electric mixer on high speed 5 minutes ➤ **1 3/4 cups sugar / 2 teaspoons vanilla / 3 large eggs**

5 Beat the melted chocolate mixture into sugar mixture with electric mixer on low speed.

6 Beat in until mixed ➤ **1 cup all-purpose flour**

7 Stir in ➤ **1 cup chopped nuts / 1 cup (6 ounces) semisweet chocolate chips, if you like**

8 Spread batter in pan.

9 Bake 40 to 45 minutes or just until brownies begin to pull away from sides of pan. Cool completely on wire rack.

10 Make ➤ **Chocolate Frosting (below)**

11 Frost brownies with frosting. Cut into 2 1/4 × 1 1/2-inch bars.

CHOCOLATE FROSTING

2-quart saucepan • Small sharp knife • Wooden spoon •
Dry-ingredient measuring cup • Measuring spoon

1 Melt in saucepan over low heat, stirring a few times, then remove from heat ▬ ▬ ▬ ▬ ▬ ▬ ▬ ▬ ➤

> **2 ounces unsweetened chocolate**
> **2 tablespoons (from a stick)**
> **margarine or butter**

2 Stir in until smooth ▬ ▬ ▬ ▬ ▬ ▬ ➤

> **2 cups powdered sugar**
> **3 tablespoons hot water**

Nutrition Per Brownie: Calories 260 (Calories from Fat 125); Fat 14g (Saturated 4g); Cholesterol 25mg; Sodium 80mg; Carbohydrate 32g (Dietary Fiber 1g); Protein 3g

DOUBLE MINT BROWNIES

24 brownies

Utensils You Will Need

Rectangular pan, 13 × 9 × 2 inches • Pastry brush • Pot holders • Spatula • Wire cooling rack • Medium bowl • Eggbeater • Liquid measuring cup • Measuring spoons • Pot holders • Ruler • Sharp knife

1 Heat oven to 350°.

2 Grease bottom only of rectangular pan with – – – – – – – – – ➤ | **Shortening**

3 Bake in pan as directed on package for fudgelike brownies – – – – – ➤ | **1 package (1 lb 6.75 oz) supreme brownie mix with pouch of chocolate flavor syrup**

4 Immediately after baking, put on brownies – – – – – – – – ➤ | **20 to 24 chocolate-covered peppermint patties, unwrapped**

5 Return brownies to oven for 3 to 4 minutes or until patties are softened.

6 Spread patties evenly over top of brownies with spatula. Cool completely on wire rack.

7 Cut into 2-inch squares. Cover and refrigerate any leftover brownies.

Nutrition Per Brownie: Calories 175 (Calories from Fat 65); Fat 7g (Saturated 1g); Cholesterol 20mg; Sodium 95mg; Carbohydrate 27g (Dietary Fiber 0g); Protein 1g

▲▲▲▲▲ SUPER SNACK BARS ▲▲▲▲▲

32 bars *(photo page 41)*

Utensils You Will Need

Large bowl • Dry-ingredient measuring cups • Small sharp knife • Measuring spoons • Wooden spoon • Rectangular pan, 13 × 9 × 2 inches • Pot holders • Wire cooling rack • Ruler • Sharp knife

1 Heat oven to 350°.

2 Grease rectangular pan with ---➤ | **Shortening**

3 Mix in large bowl with wooden spoon ---➤
| **3/4 cup granulated sugar**
| **3/4 cup packed brown sugar**
| **3/4 cup (1 1/2 sticks) margarine or butter, softened**
| **1 teaspoon vanilla**
| **2 large eggs**

4 Stir in ---➤
| **2 cups all-purpose flour**
| **1 teaspoon baking soda**
| **1/2 teaspoon baking powder**
| **1/2 teaspoon salt**
| **1 cup whole-grain wheat flake cereal, slightly crushed**
| **3/4 cup quick-cooking oats**
| **3/4 cup chopped pecans**
| **2/3 cup candy-coated chocolate candies**

5 Spread batter in pan.

6 Sprinkle with ---➤
| **1/3 cup candy-coated chocolate candies**
| **1/4 cup chopped pecans**

7 Bake 30 to 40 minutes or until golden brown. Cool completely on wire rack. Cut into about 2 × 1 1/4-inch bars.

Nutrition Per Bar: *Calories 175 (Calories from Fat 80); Fat 9g (Saturated 2g); Cholesterol 15mg; Sodium 150mg; Carbohydrate 23g (Dietary Fiber 1g); Protein 2g*

PEANUT BUTTER AND
▲▲▲▲▲ JAM BARS ▲▲▲▲▲

32 bars

Utensils You Will Need

Large bowl • Dry-ingredient measuring cups • Wooden spoon •
Measuring spoons • Tablespoon • Rectangular pan, 13 × 9 × 2 inches •
Pot holders • Wire cooling rack • Ruler • Sharp knife

1 Heat oven to 350°.

2 Mix in large bowl with wooden spoon ▶

> **1/2 cup granulated sugar**
> **1/2 cup packed brown sugar**
> **1/2 cup shortening**
> **1/2 cup peanut butter**
> **1 large egg**

3 Stir in ▶

> **1 1/4 cups all-purpose flour**
> **3/4 teaspoon baking soda**
> **1/2 teaspoon baking powder**

4 Save 1 cup dough. Press rest of the dough in rectangular pan.

5 Spread on dough in pan ▶

> **1/2 cup strawberry jam**

6 Crumble saved dough, then sprinkle over jam.

7 Bake 20 to 25 minutes or until golden brown. Cool completely on wire rack.

8 Drizzle with ▶

> **Glaze (right)**

9 Cut into about 2 × 1 1/4-inch bars.

GLAZE 1-quart saucepan • Small sharp knife •
Dry-ingredient measuring cup • Wooden spoon • Measuring spoon

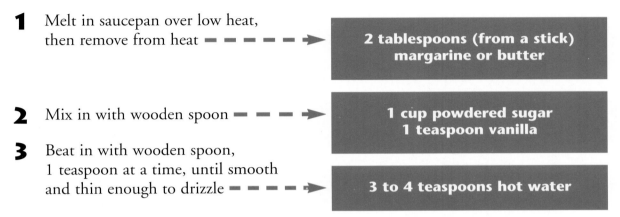

1 Melt in saucepan over low heat, then remove from heat ▸

2 tablespoons (from a stick) margarine or butter

2 Mix in with wooden spoon ▸

1 cup powdered sugar
1 teaspoon vanilla

3 Beat in with wooden spoon, 1 teaspoon at a time, until smooth and thin enough to drizzle ▸

3 to 4 teaspoons hot water

Nutrition Per Bar: *Calories 130 (Calories from Fat 55); Fat 6g (Saturated 1g); Cholesterol 10mg; Sodium 70mg; Carbohydrate 18g (Dietary Fiber 0g); Protein 1g*

HINT
You can use your favorite flavor of jam in these bars!

▲▲▲▲▲ DOUBLE APPLE BARS ▲▲▲▲▲

24 bars

Utensils You Will Need

Large bowl • Dry-ingredient measuring cups • Wooden spoon • Measuring spoons • Tablespoon • Square pan, 9 × 9 × 2 inches • Toothpick • Pot holders • Wire cooling rack • Ruler • Sharp knife

1 Heat oven to 350°.

2 Grease rectangular pan with ----➤ | **Shortening** |

3 Mix in large bowl with wooden spoon ----➤

> 3/4 cup packed brown sugar
> 3/4 cup applesauce
> 1/4 cup vegetable oil
> 1 large egg

4 Stir in ----➤

> 1 1/4 cups all-purpose flour
> 1/2 teaspoon baking soda
> 1/2 teaspoon ground cinnamon
> 1/4 teaspoon salt

5 Stir in ----➤

> 1/2 cup chopped unpeeled all-purpose apple

6 Spread batter in pan.

7 Bake 25 to 30 minutes or until toothpick poked in center comes out clean. Cool completely on wire rack.

8 If you like, sprinkle with ----➤ | **Powdered sugar** |

9 Cut into 2 1/4 × 1 1/2-inch bars.

Nutrition Per Bar: *Calories 85 (Calories from Fat 25); Fat 3g (Saturated 1g); Cholesterol 10mg; Sodium 55mg; Carbohydrate 14g (Dietary Fiber 0g); Protein 1g*

CHEWY FRUIT AND
▲▲▲▲▲ NUT BARS ▲▲▲▲▲

48 bars

Utensils You Will Need

Large bowl • Dry-ingredient measuring cups • Measuring spoons •
Wooden spoon • Jelly roll pan, 15 1/2 × 10 1/2 × 1 inches • Pot holders •
Wire cooling rack • Ruler • Sharp knife

1 Heat oven to 375°.

2 Mix in large bowl with wooden
spoon – – – – – – – – – – ▶

> **1 1/2 cups packed brown sugar**
> **1/2 cup shortening**
> **1/2 cup (1 stick) margarine or**
> **butter, softened**
> **2 large eggs**

3 Stir in – – – – – – – – ▶

> **2 cups all-purpose flour**
> **1 teaspoon baking powder**
> **1 teaspoon salt**
> **1 teaspoon ground cinnamon**

4 Stir in – – – – – – – – ▶

> **1 package (6 ounces) diced**
> **dried fruits and raisins**
> **1 cup chopped walnuts**

5 Spread batter in pan. Bake 20 to 25
minutes or until toothpick poked in
center comes out clean. Cool
completely on wire rack.

6 If you like, sprinkle with – – – ▶

> **Powdered sugar**

7 Cut into about 2 × 1 1/2-inch bars.

Nutrition Per Bar: Calories 115 (Calories from Fat 55); Fat 6g (Saturated 1g); Cholesterol 10mg; Sodium 85mg; Carbohydrate 14g (Dietary Fiber 1g); Protein 1g

Mike thought these fruity bars were easy to prepare. He also thinks they would be good with chopped dates in place of the fruit bits—we agree!

2

Creative Fun
Cakes

Chocolate Gift Loaf (page 62))

▲▲▲▲▲ HEART CAKE ▲▲▲▲▲

12 servings

🍴🥄 Utensils You Will Need

Round pan, 8 × 1 1/2 inches • Square pan, 8 × 8 × 2 inches • Pastry brush •
Liquid measuring cup • Large bowl • Electric mixer • Pot holders •
Wire cooling racks • Large tray or covered cardboard,
18 × 15 inches • Sharp knife

1 Heat oven to 350°.

2 Grease round and square pans
with ▪ ▪ ▪ ▪ ▪ ▪ ▪ ▪ ▪ ➤

> **Shortening**

3 Put small amount in pans and
shake to coat, then pour out any
extra ▪ ▪ ▪ ▪ ▪ ▪ ▪ ▪ ▪ ➤

> **All-purpose flour**

4 Make and bake as directed on
package for 8-inch round pans,
dividing batter between round and
square pans ▪ ▪ ▪ ▪ ▪ ▪ ▪ ▪ ➤

> **1 package (1 lb 2.25 oz) white
> or sour cream white cake mix
> with pudding**

5 **Adult help:** Cool cakes in pans 10
minutes, then remove from pans to
wire rack. Cool completely.

6 Cut round cake in half, as shown in drawing. Put square cake on tray with
one point toward you. Put cut side of each half of round cake against one of
the top sides of square cake, as shown in drawing, to make a heart.

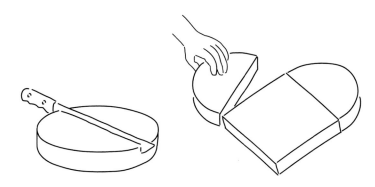

7 Make as directed on package with electric mixer ▬ ▬ ▬ ▬ ▬ ▬ ▬ ▬ ▬ ➤

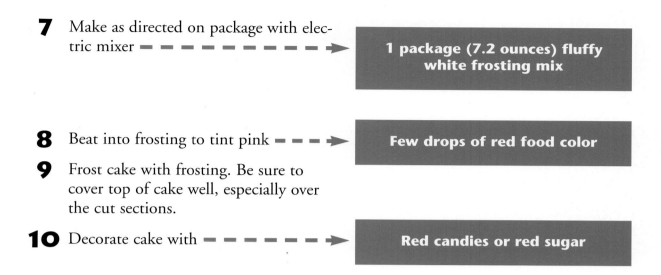

1 package (7.2 ounces) fluffy white frosting mix

8 Beat into frosting to tint pink ▬ ▬ ▬ ➤ **Few drops of red food color**

9 Frost cake with frosting. Be sure to cover top of cake well, especially over the cut sections.

10 Decorate cake with ▬ ▬ ▬ ▬ ▬ ▬ ➤ **Red candies or red sugar**

Nutrition Per Serving: *Calories 250 (Calories from Fat 25); Fat 3g (Saturated 1g); Cholesterol 0mg; Sodium 260mg; Carbohydrate 54g (Dietary Fiber 0g); Protein 2g*

▲▲▲▲▲ MYSTERY CAKE ▲▲▲▲▲

9 servings

Utensils You Will Need

Square pan, 9 × 9 × 2 inches • Pastry brush • Large bowl •
Dry-ingredient measuring cups • Measuring spoons • Electric mixer •
Rubber scraper • Toothpick • 1 1/2-quart saucepan • Small spatula

1 Heat oven to 325°.

2 Grease square pan with ▬ ▬ ▬ ▬ ➤

> **Shortening**

3 Put small amount in pan and shake to coat, then pour out any extra ▬ ▬ ▬ ➤

> **All-purpose flour**

4 Beat in large bowl with electric mixer on medium speed about 30 seconds, scraping bowl all the time, until mixed ▬ ▬ ▬ ▬ ▬ ▬ ➤

> **1 1/2 cups all-purpose flour**
> **1 cup granulated sugar**
> **2 tablespoons margarine or butter, softened**
> **1 teaspoon ground cinnamon**
> **1 teaspoon baking soda**
> **1/2 teaspoon salt**
> **1/2 teaspoon ground nutmeg**
> **1/4 teaspoon ground cloves**
> **1 large egg**
> **1 can (10 3/4 ounces) condensed tomato soup**

5 Beat batter with electric mixer on high speed 3 minutes, scraping bowl a few times.

6 If you like, stir into batter ▬ ▬ ▬ ▬ ➤

> **1/2 cup raisins**
> **1/2 cup chopped nuts**

7 Spread batter in pan.

8 Adult help: Bake 37 to 43 minutes or until toothpick poked in center comes out clean. Cool on wire rack.

9 Adult help: Heat in 1 1/2-quart saucepan over medium heat until light brown ▪ ▪ ▪ ▪ ▪ ▪ ▪ ➤

> **3 tablespoons margarine or butter**

10 Beat in ▪ ▪ ▪ ▪ ▪ ▪ ▪ ➤

> **3/4 cup powdered sugar**
> **1 teaspoon vanilla**
> **3 to 4 teaspoons milk**

11 Frost cake with frosting.

Nutrition Per Serving: *Calories 360 (Calories from Fat 110); Fat 12g (Saturated 2g); Cholesterol 25mg; Sodium 580mg; Carbohydrate 61g (Dietary Fiber 2g); Protein 4g*

HINT
Beat in enough milk to make frosting spreadable. If frosting becomes too stiff to spread, stir in more milk, 1/2 teaspoon at a time.

Clare's mom said that Clare was sure she wouldn't like this cake with tomato soup in it— but she loves it, and loves sharing the mystery!

▲▲▲▲ CHOCOLATE GIFT LOAF ▲▲▲▲

14 servings *(photo page 57)*

Utensils You Will Need

Sharp knife • Cutting board • 1-quart saucepan • Loaf pan, 9 × 5 × 3 inches •
Pastry brush • 2 large bowls • Dry-ingredient measuring cups •
Liquid measuring cup • Measuring spoons • Electric mixer • Rubber scraper •
Toothpick • Wire cooling rack • Small sharp knife • Small spatula •
Kitchen scissors

1 Heat oven to 350°.

2 Melt in saucepan over low heat,
stirring a few times, then remove
from heat and cool slightly ‑ ‑ ‑ ➤

> **2 ounces unsweetened
> chocolate, chopped**

3 Grease loaf pan with ‑ ‑ ‑ ‑ ‑ ➤

> **Shortening**

4 Put small amount in pan and shake to
coat, then pour out any extra ‑ ‑ ‑ ➤

> **All-purpose flour**

5 Beat in large bowl with electric mixer
on medium speed about 30 seconds,
scraping bowl all the time,
until mixed ‑ ‑ ‑ ‑ ‑ ‑ ‑ ‑ ‑ ➤

> **1 1/2 cups all-purpose flour
> 1 cup sugar
> 1/2 cup shortening
> 3/4 cup milk
> 2 teaspoons baking powder
> 1 teaspoon vanilla
> 1/2 teaspoon salt
> 2 large eggs
> The melted chocolate**

6 Beat batter with electric mixer on high
speed 3 minutes, scraping bowl a few
times. Spread batter in pan.

7 Bake 1 hour 5 minutes to 1 hour 10 minutes or until toothpick poked in center comes out clean. **Adult help:** Cool cake in pan 10 minutes, then remove from pan to wire rack. Cool completely.

8 Beat in second large bowl with electric mixer on medium speed until smooth and spreadable (if necessary, add more water, 1/2 teaspoon at a time) ▪ ▪ ▪ ▪ ▪ ▪ ➤

> **3 cups powdered sugar**
> **1/3 cup (from a stick)**
> **margarine or butter, softened**
> **1 teaspoon vanilla**
> **1 tablespoon water**

9 Frost cake with frosting

10 Cut into strips with scissors, and put on cake to look like ribbon on a wrapped package, looping strips on top for bow ▪ ▪ ▪ ▪ ▪ ▪ ➤

> **2 rolls cherry or strawberry**
> **chewy fruit snack (from 4-ounce**
> **package)**

Nutrition Per Serving: Calories 370 (Calories from Fat 145); Fat 16g (Saturated 5g); Cholesterol 60 mg; Sodium 210mg; Carbohydrate 54g; (Dietary Fiber 1g); Protein 3g

Amanda enjoyed the step-by-step process of making this special cake. Her family thought it looked very attractive, and she was pleased by their reaction.

COOKIE-SOUR CREAM CAKE

8 servings

Utensils You Will Need

Round pan, 8 × 1 1/2 or 9 × 1 1/2 inches • Pastry brush • Sharp knife •
Cutting board • Large bowl • Dry-ingredient measuring cup •
Small sharp knife • Liquid measuring cup • Measuring spoons •
Electric mixer • Rubber scraper • Wooden spoon • Pot holders •
Wire cooling rack

1 Heat oven to 350°.

2 Grease round pan with ▬ ▬ ▬ ▬ ▶ | **Shortening**

3 Put small amount in pan and shake
to coat, then pour out any extra ▬ ▬ ▶ | **All-purpose flour**

4 **Adult help:** Coarsely chop with knife,
then set aside ▬ ▬ ▬ ▬ ▬ ▬ ▶ | **8 creme-filled sandwich cookies**

5 Beat in large bowl with electric
mixer on low speed 30 seconds,
scraping bowl all the time ▬ ▬ ▬ ▬ ▶

6 Beat batter with electric mixer on high
speed 2 minutes, scraping bowl a few
times. Stir the chopped cookies into
batter. Spread batter in pan.

> **1 cup all-purpose flour**
> **3/4 cup sugar**
> **1/2 cup sour cream**
> **1/4 cup (1/2 stick) margarine**
> **or butter, softened**
> **1/4 cup water**
> **1/2 teaspoon baking soda**
> **1/2 teaspoon baking powder**
> **1 large egg**

7 Bake 30 to 35 minutes or until cake
springs back when touched lightly in
center. **Adult help:** Cool cake in pan
10 minutes, then remove from pan to
wire rack. (See right.) Cool completely.

8 Frost cake with ▬ ▬ ▬ ▬ ▬ ▶ | **Sweetened Whipped Cream
(right)**

9 If you like, decorate cake with more
cookies.

Help for step 7.

SWEETENED WHIPPED CREAM Medium

bowl • Liquid measuring cup • Measuring spoon • Eggbeater

1   Chill medium bowl in freezer about 15 minutes or until cold.

2   Beat in chilled bowl with eggbeater until stiff - - - - - - - - - - →

> **3/4 cup whipping (heavy) cream**
> **2 tablespoons granulated or powdered sugar**

Nutrition Per Serving: Calories 340 (Calories from Fat 160); Fat 18g (Saturated 8g); Cholesterol 60mg; Sodium 250mg; Carbohydrate 42g (Dietary Fiber 1g); Protein 4g

Sara thought frosting and decorating cake with cookies was almost as much fun as eating it! She suggests using frozen whipped topping (thawed) for the frosting in place of the whipped cream. We think that would work just great.

UPSIDE-DOWN ▲▲▲▲ PINEAPPLE CAKE ▲▲▲▲

9 servings *(photo page 68)*

Utensils You Will Need

Square pan, 9 × 9 × 2 inches • Small sharp knife • Pot holders •
Dry-ingredient measuring cups • Can opener • Large bowl •
Liquid measuring cup • Measuring spoons • Electric mixer •
Rubber scraper • Toothpick • Heatproof serving plate

1 Heat oven to 350°.

2 Melt in square pan in oven ▸ | **1/4 cup (1/2 stick) margarine or butter**

3 Sprinkle over margarine ▸ | **2/3 cup packed brown sugar**

4 Put on top of brown sugar mixture ▸ | **1 can (about 16 ounces) sliced pineapple, drained**

5 If you like, put in centers of pineapple slices ▸ | **Maraschino cherries**

6 Beat in large bowl with electric mixer on low speed 30 seconds, scraping bowl all the time ▸ | **1 1/3 cups all-purpose flour**
1 cup granulated sugar
1/3 cup shortening
3/4 cup milk
1 1/2 teaspoons baking powder
1/2 teaspoon salt
1 large egg

7 Beat batter with electric mixer on high speed 3 minutes, scraping bowl a few times. Pour batter over fruit mixture in pan.

8 Bake 55 to 60 minutes or until toothpick poked in center comes out clean. **Adult help:** Immediately turn pan upside down onto heatproof serving plate. Let pan remain over cake a few minutes, then remove pan.

9 Serve warm, and if you like, serve with ▬ ▬ ▬ ▬ ▬ ▬ ▬ ▬ ▬ ➤

> **Sweetened Whipped Cream (page 65)**

Nutrition Per Serving: Calories 440 (Calories from Fat 180); Fat 20g (Saturated 7g); Cholesterol 45mg; Sodium 290mg; Carbohydrate 62g (Dietary Fiber 1g); Protein 4g

HINT
If any pieces of pineapple or cherries stick to the pan when you remove it, just pick them off and place on cake where they go.

▲▲▲▲ CANDY BAR CUPCAKES ▲▲▲▲

About 20 cupcakes

 Utensils You Will Need

Muffin pan with medium cups, 2 1/2 × 1 1/4 inches • Pastry brush •
Cutting board • Sharp knife • Large bowl • Liquid measuring cup •
Electric mixer • Pot holders • Wire cooling rack

1 **Adult help:** Coarsely chop all the
candy, then finely chop enough to
measure 3/4 cup ▬ ▬ ▬ ▬ ▬ ▬ ▶

> **8 bars (2.1 ounces each)
> chocolate-covered crispy
> peanut-buttery candy**

2 Make and bake cupcakes as directed on
package—except after beating, gently
stir in the 3/4 cup finely chopped
candy ▬ ▬ ▬ ▬ ▬ ▬ ▬ ▶

> **1 package (1 lb 2.25 oz) white
> cake mix with pudding**

3 **Adult help:** Immediately remove
cupcakes from pan to wire rack.
Cool completely.

4 Frost cupcakes with ▬ ▬ ▬ ▬ ▶

> **1 tub (1 lb) milk chocolate
> ready-to-spread frosting**

5 Put coarsely chopped candy pieces
on tops of cupcakes. Store loosely covered at room
temperature.

*Nutrition Per Cupcake: Calories 330 (Calories from
Fat 135); Fat 15g (Saturated 10g); Cholesterol 5mg;
Sodium 250mg; Carbohydrate 46g (Dietary Fiber 1g);
Protein 4g*

HINT
*Candy bars are
easier to cut if
refrigerated
about 1 hour.*

Upside-down Pineapple Cake (page 66)

BANANA-OATMEAL CAKE

15 servings

Utensils You Will Need

Rectangular pan, 13 × 9 × 2 inches • Pastry brush • Large bowl •
Liquid measuring cup • Dry-ingredient measuring cups • Fork •
Measuring spoons • Wooden spoon • Pot holders • Toothpick •
Wire cooling rack

1 Heat oven to 350°.

2 Grease rectangular pan with - - - →

> **Shortening**

3 Beat in large bowl with wooden spoon - - - - - - - →

> 1 1/2 cups mashed very ripe
> bananas (4 medium)
> 3/4 cup sugar
> 2/3 cup vegetable oil
> 2/3 cup buttermilk
> 1 teaspoon vanilla
> 1 large egg

4 Mix in - - - - - - - →

> 1 1/3 cups all-purpose flour
> 1 cup quick-cooking or regular
> oats
> 2 teaspoons baking soda
> 1 1/2 teaspoons ground
> cinnamon
> 1 teaspoon baking powder
> 1/2 teaspoon ground cloves

5 Stir in - - - - - - - →

> 2/3 cup chopped nuts
> 2/3 cup raisins

6 Spread batter in pan.

7 Bake 30 to 35 minutes or until toothpick poked in center comes out clean. Cool completely on wire rack.

8 If you like, sprinkle with ▬ ▬ ▬ ▬ ➤ | **Powdered sugar**

Nutrition Per Serving: *Calories 275 (Calories from Fat 125); Fat 14g (Saturated 2g); Cholesterol 15mg; Sodium 220mg; Carbohydrate 35g (Dietary Fiber 2g); Protein 4g*

Kirsten thought it was fun for a kid like her to make a cake all by herself and let people try it. She chose to leave the raisins out.

▲▲▲▲▲ JELLY ROLL ▲▲▲▲▲

10 servings

Utensils You Will Need

Jelly roll pan, 15 1/2 × 10 1/2 × 1 inch • Aluminum foil • Pastry brush •
Medium mixer bowl • Electric mixer • Dry-ingredient measuring cups •
Liquid measuring cup • Measuring spoons • Toothpick • Pot holders •
Clean kitchen towel • Sharp knife • Wire cooling rack • Fork • Knife

1 Heat oven to 375°. Line jelly roll pan with aluminum foil.

2 Generously grease foil with ▬ ▬ ▬ ➤ | **Shortening**

3 Beat in medium bowl with electric mixer on high speed about 5 minutes or until thick and lemon-colored ▬ ➤ | **3 large eggs**

4 Beat in, a little at a time ▬ ▬ ▬ ➤ | **1 cup granulated sugar**

5 Beat in on low speed ▬ ▬ ▬ ▬ ➤ | **1/3 cup water**
1 teaspoon vanilla

6 Beat in, a little at a time, just until batter is smooth ▬ ▬ ▬ ▬ ➤ | **1 cup cake flour or 3/4 cup all-purpose flour**
1 teaspoon baking powder
1/4 teaspoon salt

7 Pour batter into pan, spreading to corners.

8 Bake 12 to 15 minutes or until toothpick poked in center comes out clean.

9 Sprinkle towel generously with ▬ ▬ ➤ | **Powdered sugar**

10 **Adult help:** Immediately after baking, loosen cake from edges of pan and turn upside down onto towel. Carefully remove foil. Trim off edges of cake if they are very crisp so that cake will not split when rolled.

11 **Adult help:** While hot, carefully roll cake and towel from narrow end. Cool on wire rack at least 30 minutes. Unroll cake and remove towel.

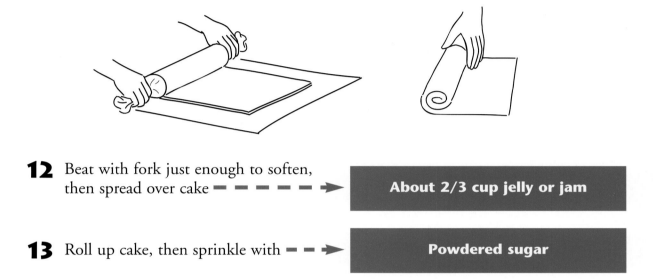

12 Beat with fork just enough to soften, then spread over cake ▪ ▪ ▪ ▪ ▪ ➤ | About 2/3 cup jelly or jam

13 Roll up cake, then sprinkle with ▪ ▪ ▪ ➤ | Powdered sugar

Nutrition Per Serving: Calories 215 (Calories from Fat 20); Fat 2g (Saturated 1g); Cholesterol 65 mg; Sodium 130mg; Carbohydrate 46g (Dietary Fiber 0g); Protein 3g

Justin was very pleased with his finished cake and thought it looked like something from a bakery— and it tasted good too!

▲▲▲▲▲ MINIATURE LOGS ▲▲▲▲▲

About 14 logs

🍴 Utensils You Will Need

Large bowl • Liquid measuring cups • Rubber scraper •
Muffin pan with medium cups, 2 1/2 × 1 1/4 inches • Pastry brush •
Pot holders • Wire cooling rack • Knife • Fork • Rolling pin • Sharp knife

1 Make and bake 28 cupcakes as
directed on ▬ ▬ ▬ ▬ ▬ ▬ ▬ ▶

> **1 package (1 lb 2.25 oz) devil's food cake mix with pudding**

2 **Adult help:** Immediately remove cupcakes from pan to wire rack. Cool completely.

3 Remove paper baking cups if you
used them.

4 Make ▬ ▬ ▬ ▬ ▬ ▬ ▬ ▶

> **Creamy Chocolate Frosting (right)**

5 Put 2 cupcakes together end to end, as
shown in drawing, with a small amount
of frosting. Frost sides of logs, leaving
ends unfrosted. Make strokes in frosting
with fork to look like bark.

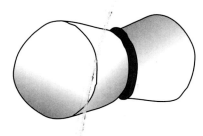

6 Sprinkle generously on breadboard ▬ ▶

> **Sugar**

7 Roll in sugar into 1/8-inch-thick
ovals ▬ ▬ ▬ ▬ ▬ ▬ ▬ ▶

> **14 large red gumdrops**

8 Cut hatchets from ovals, as shown in drawing. Wipe kitchen knife on wet sponge between hatchets. Put a gumdrop hatchet on each log.

CREAMY CHOCOLATE FROSTING

1-quart saucepan • Wooden spoon • Large bowl • Electric mixer • Dry-ingredient measuring cups • Measuring spoons

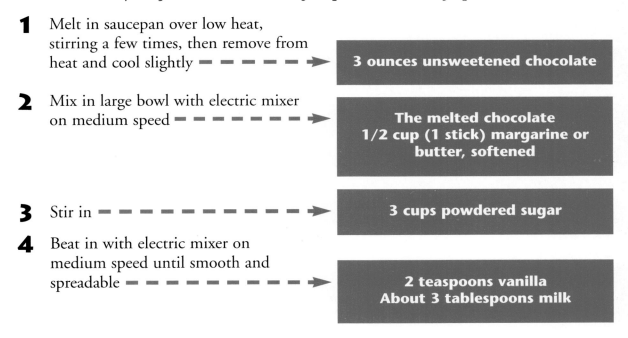

1 Melt in saucepan over low heat, stirring a few times, then remove from heat and cool slightly ▪ ▪ ▪ ▪ ▪ ➤ | **3 ounces unsweetened chocolate**

2 Mix in large bowl with electric mixer on medium speed ▪ ▪ ▪ ▪ ▪ ➤ | **The melted chocolate**
1/2 cup (1 stick) margarine or butter, softened

3 Stir in ▪ ▪ ▪ ▪ ▪ ▪ ➤ | **3 cups powdered sugar**

4 Beat in with electric mixer on medium speed until smooth and spreadable ▪ ▪ ▪ ▪ ▪ ➤ | **2 teaspoons vanilla**
About 3 tablespoons milk

Nutrition Per Log: *Calories 355 (Calories from Fat 115); Fat 13g (Saturated 4g); Cholesterol 0mg; Sodium 410mg; Carbohydrate 60g (Dietary Fiber 2g); Protein 2g*

3

Nifty Pizzas and Big Breads

Top-It-Your-Way Pizza (page 78)

▲▲▲▲▲ TOP-IT-YOUR-WAY PIZZA ▲▲▲▲▲

4 servings

Utensils You Will Need

Cookie sheet or pizza pan, 15 inches • Pastry brush • Ruler • Can opener • Rubber scraper • Sharp knife • Cutting board • Dry-ingredient measuring cups • Pot holders • Wire cooling rack • Pizza cutter

1 Move oven rack to lowest position. Heat oven to 350°.

2 Grease cookie sheet or pizza pan with – – – – – – – – ➤

> **Shortening**

3 Thaw as directed on package, then shape into 14 × 11-inch rectangle on cookie sheet or 14-inch circle on pizza pan – – – – – – – – ➤

> **1 loaf (1 pound) frozen pizza dough**

4 Spread over dough with rubber scraper – – – – – – – – ➤

> **1 can (8 ounces) pizza sauce**

5 Choose 2 or 3 of these toppings, and sprinkle them over the sauce – ➤

> **1 cup sliced mushrooms**
> **1/2 cup chopped green bell pepper**
> **1/4 cup sliced ripe olives**
> **A few thinly sliced onion rings**
> **1/2 package (3 1/2-ounce size) thinly sliced pepperoni**
> **1/4 pound hamburger or sausage, cooked**
> **Other favorite topping**

6 Sprinkle over the toppings ▬ ▬ ▬ ▬ ➤ **1 1/2 cups shredded mozzarella cheese (6 ounces)**

7 Bake on lowest oven rack 25 to 35 minutes or until cheese is melted and light brown. Cut pizza into wedges.

Nutrition Per Serving: *Calories 510 (Calories from Fat 225); Fat 25g (Saturated 9g); Cholesterol 50mg; Sodium 1170mg; Carbohydrate 49g (Dietary Fiber 4g); Protein 26g*

HINT
*Any combination
of your favorite pizza
toppings will work*

POCKET PIZZA

2 servings

Utensils You Will Need

Cookie sheet • Pastry brush • Small bowl • Dry-ingredient measuring cups •
Liquid measuring cup • Measuring spoons • Wooden spoon •
Rolling pin • Ruler • Scissors • Fork • Pot holders

1 Stir hard in small bowl with wooden spoon until dough leaves side of bowl (if dough seems dry, add 1 to 2 tablespoons milk) – – – ➤

> **1 cup all-purpose flour**
> **1/3 cup milk**
> **2 tablespoons vegetable oil**
> **I teaspoon baking powder**
> **1/2 teaspoon salt**

2 Sprinkle a clean surface (such as a kitchen counter or breadboard) with flour. Put dough on surface. Roll ball of dough around 3 or 4 times. Knead dough quickly and lightly by folding, pressing and turning. Repeat 10 times. Cover dough with bowl and let stand 15 minutes.

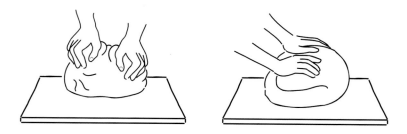

3 Heat oven to 425°.

4 Grease cookie sheet with – – – – ➤ **Shortenimg**

5 Roll or pat dough into 12-inch circle on lightly floured surface. Fold dough loosely in half. Put dough on cookie sheet, then unfold.

6 Brush dough lightly, using pastry brush, with ▪ ▪ ▪ ▪ ▪ ▪ ▪ ▶

> **Vegetable oil**

7 Layer on half of the dough circle in the order listed ▪ ▪ ▪ ▪ ▪ ▪ ▶

8 Fold dough over filling. Turn edge of lower dough over edge of top dough, then pinch edge to seal. Poke top with fork.

9 Bake 20 to 25 minutes or until golden brown. Cut pizza in half.

> 1/4 cup pizza sauce
> 1/2 cup shredded mozzarella cheese (2 ounces)
> 1 tablespoon finely chopped onion or 1/4 teaspoon onion powder
> 1/8 to 1/4 teaspoon garlic powder
> About 1/2 package (3 1/2-ounce size) thinly sliced pepperoni
> 2 to 3 tablespoons pizza sauce
> Another 1/2 cup shredded mozzarella cheese (2 ounces)

Here's another idea. . . Make **Pocket Ham and Cheese Sandwich**: Use barbecue sauce in place of the pizza sauce, Monterey Jack cheese in place of the mozzarella cheese and 3/4 cup diced fully cooked smoked ham in place of the Italian sausage. Leave out pepperoni.

Nutrition Per Serving: Calories 785 (Calories from Fat 430); Fat 48g (Saturated 15g); Cholesterol 70mg; Sodium 1860mg; Carbohydrate 57g (Dietary Fiber 3g); Protein 34g

Caitlin says she'd make this recipe again because it tastes very good and looks impressive, but is easy to make. She suggests using a fork to seal the dough to make cute little ridges along the edge.

▲▲▲▲ PIZZA BITES ▲▲▲▲

6 servings

Utensils You Will Need

Toaster • Small bowl • Small sharp knife • Measuring spoons • Spoon •
Sharp knife • Cutting board • Cookie sheet • Dry-ingredient
measuring cup • Pot holders

1 Heat oven to 425°.

2 Split with fork, then toast ‑ ‑ ‑ ‑ ➤ | **3 English muffins**

3 Mix in small bowl with spoon,
then spread on muffin halves ‑ ‑ ‑ ➤ | **2 tablespoons margarine or butter, softened**
1/8 teaspoon instant minced garlic

4 Cut each muffin half into 4 wedges.
Put wedges, with sides touching, on
cookie sheet.

5 Put 1 slice on each muffin wedge ‑ ➤ | **About 1/2 package (3 1/2-ounce size) thinly sliced pepperoni**

6 Sprinkle over muffin wedges ‑ ‑ ‑ ➤ | **1 cup shredded mozzarella cheese (4 ounces)**
1/2 teaspoon dried oregano leaves

7 Bake 8 to 10 minutes or until cheese is
melted. Separate into wedges.

Nutrition Per Serving: Calories 175 (Calories from Fat 90); Fat 10g (Saturated 4g); Cholesterol 15mg; Sodium 340mg; Carbohydrate 14g (Dietary Fiber 1g); Protein 8g

**These easy pizza treats were a hit with Will.
He plans to make them when he invites friends
for a sleepover.**

Apple-Cinnamon Bread (page 84)

APPLE-CINNAMON ▲▲▲▲▲ BREAD ▲▲▲▲▲

1 loaf (16 slices) *(photo page 83)*

Utensils You Will Need

Loaf pan, 9 × 5 × 3 inches • Pastry brush • Cutting board • Sharp knives • Large bowl • Dry-ingredient measuring cups • Measuring spoons • Wooden spoon • Small bowl • Pot holders • Toothpick • Wire cooling rack

1 Heat oven to 350°.

2 Grease bottom only of loaf pan with ----→ **Shortening**

3 **Adult help:** Cut into fourths, then core, peel and chop to measure 2 cups ----→ **About 2 medium cooking apples**

4 Mix in large bowl with wooden spoon ----→
1 cup sugar
1/2 cup shortening
1 teaspoon vanilla
2 large eggs

5 Stir in until smooth (batter will be thick) ----→
2 cups all-purpose flour
1 teaspoon baking powder
1 teaspoon baking soda
1 teaspoon ground cinnamon
1/2 teaspoon salt

6 Stir in ----→
The chopped apples
1/2 cup chopped walnuts
1/2 cup raisins

7 Spread batter in pan.

8 Mix in small bowl, then sprinkle over batter ➤

| 1 tablespoon sugar |
| 1/4 teaspoon ground cinnamon |

9 Bake 50 to 55 minutes or until toothpick poked about 1 inch from center comes out clean. **Adult help:** Immediately remove bread from pan to wire rack. Cool. Store bread tightly covered.

Nutrition Per Slice: Calories 235 (Calories from Fat 90); Fat 10g (Saturated 2g); Cholesterol 25mg; Sodium 190mg; Carbohydrate 35g (Dietary Fiber 2g); Protein 3g

Joey learned something new while making this bread—how to chop apples, which he thought was lots of fun. To suit his tastes, he made a simple change to the recipe and left the nuts out.

▲▲▲▲▲ CORN BREAD ▲▲▲▲▲

12 servings

🍴 Utensils You Will Need

Round pan, 9 × 1 1/2 inches, or square pan, 8 × 8 × 2 inches • Pastry brush •
Large bowl • Dry-ingredient measuring cups • Liquid measuring cup •
Measuring spoons • Wooden spoon • Pot holders • Wire cooling rack

1 Heat oven to 450°.

2 Grease round or square pan with ━ ➤ **Shortening**

3 Mix in large bowl with wooden spoon ━ ━ ━ ━ ━ ━ ━ ➤

4 Beat batter hard with spoon 30 seconds. Spread batter in pan.

5 Bake 25 to 30 minutes or until golden brown. Cool slightly on wire rack. Serve warm.

> 1 1/2 cups yellow or white corn-meal
> 1/2 cup all-purpose flour
> 1 1/2 cups buttermilk
> 1/4 cup vegetable oil
> 2 teaspoons baking powder
> 1 teaspoon sugar
> 1 teaspoon salt
> 1/2 teaspoon baking soda
> 2 large eggs

Here's another idea. . . Make **Corn Muffins**: Use muffin pan with medium cups, 2 1/2 × 1 1/4 inches. Grease 14 muffin cups with shortening, or line muffin cups with paper baking cups. Spoon batter into muffin cups until almost to top. Bake about 20 minutes. Makes 14 muffins.

Nutrition Per Slice: Calories 150 (Calories from Fat 55); Fat 6g (Saturated 1g); Cholesterol 35mg; Sodium 350mg; Carbohydrate 20g (Dietary Fiber 1g); Protein 4g

Turtle Bread (page 88)

▲▲▲▲▲ TURTLE BREAD ▲▲▲▲▲

16 slices *(photo page 87)*

Utensils You Will Need

Large bowl • Dry-ingredient measuring cups • Measuring spoons • Wooden spoon • 1-quart saucepan • Liquid measuring cup • Clean kitchen towel • Small sharp knife • Cookie sheet • Pastry brush • Sharp knife • Pot holders • Wire cooling rack

1 Mix in large bowl with wooden spoon ▪ ▪ ▪ ▪ ▪ ▪ ▪ ▪ ▶

> **1 1/2 cups all-purpose flour**
> **1 package quick-acting active dry yeast**
> **1 tablespoon sugar**
> **1 teaspoon salt**

2 Heat in saucepan until very warm, then stir into yeast mixture ▪ ▪ ▪ ▶

> **1/2 cup water**
> **1/3 cup milk**
> **1 tablespoon (from a stick) margarine or butter**

3 Stir in ▪ ▪ ▪ ▪ ▪ ▪ ▪ ▪ ▪ ▶

> **1 large egg**

4 Stir in enough to make dough easy to handle ▪ ▪ ▪ ▪ ▪ ▪ ▪ ▶

> **1 to 1 1/2 cups all-purpose flour**

5 Sprinkle a clean surface (such as a kitchen counter or breadboard) with flour. Put dough on surface. Roll ball of dough around 3 or 4 times. Knead dough quickly and lightly by folding, pressing and turning. Continue kneading about 5 minutes or until dough is smooth and elastic. Cover dough with towel and let rest 10 minutes.

6 Lightly grease cookie sheet with ▪ ▪ ▶

> **Shortening**

7 Shape a 2-inch piece of dough into a ball for turtle's head. Shape four 1 1/2-inch pieces of dough into balls for turtle's feet. Shape one 1 1/2-inch piece of dough into turtle's tail. Shape remaining dough into a ball for turtle's body.

8 Put body on cookie sheet and flatten slightly. Put balls of dough for head, feet and tail around body. Stick one end of each ball under edge of body to attach.

9 Press into head for eyes ▬ ▬ ▬ ▬ ▬ ▶ **2 raisins**

10 Cover turtle with towel and let rise in warm place 20 minutes.

11 Heat oven to 400°.

12 **Adult help:** Make crisscross cuts, 1/4 inch deep, in turtle's body to make it look like a turtle's shell, using sharp knife.

13 Bake 20 to 25 minutes or until golden brown. **Adult help:** Remove turtle from cookie sheet to wire rack. Cool.

14 If you like, for a shiny surface, brush baked turtle with ▬ ▬ ▬ ▬ ▬ ▶ **Margarine or butter, softened**

Here's another idea. . . Make **Shaped Bread:** Dough can be shaped into an alligator, bear, cow, dog, doll, ladybug, pretzel, snake, snowman or whatever. Cover shape and let rise 20 minutes. Cut an X shape in dough for eyes, nose, buttons or whatever you like, using kitchen scissors, if desired. Bake as directed. Cool bread. Then decorate with raisins, currants, chocolate chips or whatever you like, attaching to bread with a drop of honey.

Nutrition Per Slice: Calories 90 (Calories from Fat 20); Fat 2g (Saturated 1g); Cholesterol 15mg; Sodium 160mg; Carbohydrate 16g (Dietary Fiber 1g); Protein 3g

EASY BREAD FIX-UPS

Tasty, toasty English muffins, bagels and breads make a great breakfast treat, snack or add-on to your favorite soup or pasta dish. Flavored with lemon, caramel and coconut, raisins and peanut butter or cinnamon, you're sure to fine a favorite that you'll want to make often.

LEMON ENGLISH MUFFINS   8 muffin rounds

Set oven control to broil. In small bowl, mix 1/4 cup margarine or butter, softened, 1 tablespoon honey and 1/2 teaspoon grated lemon peel in small bowl.

Spread margarine mixture on 4 English muffins that have been split open. Place muffin halves, margarine sides up, on rack in broiler pan. Toast 4 inches from heat 2 to 3 minutes or until golden brown (watch carefully).

CARAMEL-COCONUT BAGELS   2 bagel rounds

Set oven control to broil. In small bowl, mix 2 tablespoons packed brown sugar, 2 tablespoons flaked coconut and 1 tablespoon margarine or butter, softened with spoon.

Spread margarine mixture on 1 bagel that has been split open. Place bagel halves, margarine sides up, on rack in broiler pan. Toast 4 inches from heat 2 to 3 minutes or until golden brown (watch carefully).

CINNAMON TOAST   8 strips toast

In small bowl, mix 2 tablespoons sugar and 1 teaspoon ground cinnamon with spoon. Spread cinnamon mixture on 2 pieces hot buttered toast. Cut each piece of toast into 4 strips.

RAISIN-PEANUT BUTTER TOAST   8 triangles toast

Mix 1/4 cup peanut butter, 2 tablespoons chopped raisins and 2 tablespoons orange juice in small bowl with spoon. Spread peanut butter mixture on 2 pieces hot buttered toast. Cut each piece of toast into 4 triangles.

Toast Toppings: Lemon English Muffins, Caramel-Coconut Bagels, Cinnamon Toast, Raisin Peanut Butter Toast

CALICO BATTER BREAD

1 loaf (16 slices)

Utensils You Will Need

2 Large bowls • Dry-ingredient measuring cups • Measuring spoons • Wooden spoon • Liquid measuring cup • Electric mixer • Rubber scraper • Kitchen towels • Loaf pan, 8 1/2 × 4 1/2 × 2 1/2 or 9 × 5 × 3 inches • Pot holders • Wire cooling rack • Pastry brush

1 Mix in large bowl with wooden spoon ------→

> **2 cups all-purpose flour**
> **2 tablespoons sugar**
> **1 teaspoon salt**
> **1 package regular or quick-acting active dry yeast**

2 Add to yeast mixture, then beat with electric mixer on low speed 30 seconds, scraping bowl all the time ------→

> **1 1/4 cups very warm water**
> **2 tablespoons shortening**

3 Beat batter with electric mixer on medium speed 2 minutes, scraping bowl a few times. Pour half of the batter into another large bowl.

4 Stir into one half of batter, scraping batter from side of bowl, until smooth ------→

> **1/2 cup all-purpose flour**

5 Stir into other half of batter, scraping batter from side of bowl, until smooth ------→

> **1/2 cup whole wheat flour**

6 Cover each bowl of batter with towel and let rise in warm place 30 to 45 minutes or until batters double.

7 Grease loaf pan with ------→

> **Shortening**

8 Stir down batters by beating each 25 strokes with wooden spoon. Spoon some of one batter into pan, then spoon some of the other batter into pan. Repeat until all batter is used up. (Batters will be sticky.) Smooth out top of loaf by patting batter into shape with floured hand.

9 Cover and let rise in warm place about 45 minutes or until batter is 1/4 inch from top of 8 1/2-inch pan or 1 inch from top of 9-inch pan.

10 Heat oven to 375°.

11 Bake 40 to 45 minutes or until bread is deep golden brown and sounds hollow when tapped. **Adult help:** Immediately remove bread from pan to wire rack.

12 Brush top of loaf, using pastry brush, with ▬ ▬ ▬ ▬ ▬ ▬ ▬ ➤ **Margarine or butter, softened**

Nutrition Per Slice: Calories 105 (Calories from Fat 25); Fat 3g (Saturated 1g); Cholesterol 0mg; Sodium 140mg; Carbohydrate 19g (Dietary Fiber 1g); Protein 2g

Charlie was surprised and delighted at how easy this bread was to make. He said it tasted so good his family ate the whole loaf without putting anything on it, and the marbled design was fun to cut into!

▲▲▲▲▲ EASY CINNAMON ROLLS ▲▲▲▲▲

12 rolls

Utensils You Will Need

Muffin pan with medium cups, 2 1/2 × 1 1/4 inches • Pastry brush • 2 small bowls • Fork • Dry-ingredient measuring cups • Liquid measuring cup • Rubber spatula • Rolling pin • Ruler • Knife • Teaspoon • Measuring spoons • Sharp knife • Pot holders • Wire cooling rack

1 Heat oven to 425°.

2 Grease 12 muffin cups with - - - ➤ | **Shortening**

3 Mix in small bowl with fork to make a soft dough - - - ➤ | **2 cups Bisquick Original baking mix** / **2/3 cup milk**

4 Sprinkle a clean surface (such as a kitchen counter or breadboard) with flour or baking mix. Put dough on surface. Roll ball of dough around 3 or 4 times. Knead dough quickly and lightly by folding, pressing and turning. Repeat 10 times. Roll or pat dough into 12 × 7-inch rectangle.

5 Spread dough with - - - - - ➤ | **Margarine or butter, softened**

6 Mix in small bowl, then sprinkle over dough - - - - - ➤ | **1/4 cup sugar** / **1 teaspoon ground cinnamon**

7 Roll dough up tightly, starting at the long end of the rectangle. Pinch edge of dough into roll to seal. Cut dough into 1-inch slices. Put each slice in a muffin cup.

8 Bake about 15 minutes or until brown. **Adult help:** Remove rolls from muffin cups to wire rack. Cool.

Nutrition Per Roll: *Calories 110 (Calories from Fat 35); Fat 4g (Saturated 1g); Cholesterol 5mg; Sodium 300mg; Carbohydrate 17g (Dietary Fiber 0g); Protein 2g*

Pull-apart Coffee Cake (page 96)

▲▲▲▲ PULL-APART COFFEE CAKE ▲▲▲▲

16 servings

Utensils You Will Need

1-quart saucepan • Liquid measuring cup • 2 large bowls • Kitchen scissors •
Wooden spoon • Dry-ingredient measuring cups • Small sharp knife •
Measuring spoons • Kitchen towel • Ruler • Small bowl • Tube pan,
10 × 4 inches • Pastry brush • Pot holders • Serving plate • 2 forks

1 Mix in large bowl with wooden
spoon ----➤

> **2 cups all-purpose flour**
> **1/3 cup sugar**
> **1 teaspoon salt**
> **1 package regular or quick-acting active dry yeast**

2 Heat in saucepan until very warm --➤

> **1/2 cup milk**
> **1/2 cup warm water**

3 Stir into yeast mixture, then beat
with wooden spoon until smooth --➤

> **The warm milk mixture**
> **1/3 cup shortening or margarine or butter (from a stick), softened**
> **1 egg**

4 Mix in enough to make dough
easy to handle ----➤

> **1 1/2 to 2 cups all-purpose flour**

5 Sprinkle a clean surface (such as a
kitchen counter or breadboard) with flour. Put dough on surface. Roll ball
of dough around 3 or 4 times. Knead dough quickly and lightly by folding,
pressing and turning. Continue kneading about 5 minutes or until dough is
smooth and elastic.

6 Grease large bowl with ----➤

> **Shortening**

7 Put dough in bowl, then turn greased side up. Cover dough with towel and let rise in warm place about 1 1/2 hours or until dough doubles. (Dough is ready if a mark stays when dough is touched.)

8 Grease tube pan with ━ ━ ━ ━ ━ ━ ➤ | **Shortening**

9 Mix in small bowl ━ ━ ━ ━ ━ ━ ➤ | **3/4 cup sugar**
1/2 cup finely chopped nuts
1 teaspoon ground cinnamon

10 Melt in saucepan over low heat ━ ━ ➤ | **1/2 cup (1 stick) margarine or butter**

11 Punch down dough with fist. Shape dough into 1 1/2-inch balls.

12 Dip each ball in margarine, then in sugar-nut mixture. Put a single layer of balls in pan so they just touch. (If pan has removable bottom, line with aluminum foil.) Top with another layer of balls. Cover and let rise in warm place about 40 minutes or until balls double.

13 Heat oven to 375°.

14 Bake 35 to 40 minutes or until golden brown. (If coffee cake browns too quickly, cover loosely with aluminum foil.) **Adult help:** Loosen coffee cake from pan. Immediately turn pan upside down onto serving plate. Let pan stay a minute so margarine-sugar mixture can drizzle over coffee cake, then remove pan. Serve coffee cake while warm by pulling it apart with fingers or breaking apart with 2 forks.

Nutrition Per Serving: Calories 275 (Calories from Fat 115); Fat 13g (Saturated 3g); Cholesterol 15mg; Sodium 210mg; Carbohydrate 36g (Dietary Fiber 1g); Protein 4g

This cake reminded Mike of cinnamon buns! He learned how to knead dough, which he thought was easy once his mom showed him how. The hardest part? Waiting for the dough to rise.

4

▲▲▲▲▲▲

Munchable Muffins and Mini-Breads

Cheesy Pretzels (page 116), Blueberry Streusel Muffins (page 100)

BLUEBERRY STREUSEL
▲▲▲▲▲ **MUFFINS** ▲▲▲▲▲

12 muffins

Utensils You Will Need

Small bowl • Dry-ingredient measuring cups • Measuring spoons •
Fork • Small sharp knife • Wooden spoon •
Muffin pan with medium cups, 2 1/2 × 1 1/4 inches • Pastry brush •
Medium bowl • Liquid measuring cup • Pot holders • Wire cooling rack

1 Heat oven to 400°.

2 For topping, mix in small bowl with fork until crumbly, then set aside ▬ ▬ ▬ ▬ ▶

> 1/4 cup all-purpose flour
> 2 tablespoons packed brown sugar
> 2 tablespoons firm margarine or butter
> 1/4 teaspoon ground cinnamon

3 Grease bottoms only of 12 muffin cups with (or line muffin cups with paper baking cups) ▬ ▬ ▬ ▬ ▶

> Shortening

4 Beat in medium bowl with fork ▬ ▬ ▶

> 1 cup milk
> 1/4 cup vegetable oil
> 1/2 teaspoon vanilla
> 1 large egg

5 Stir into milk mixture just until all the flour is wet (do not stir too much—batter will be lumpy) ▬ ▬ ▶

> 2 cups all-purpose or whole wheat flour
> 1/3 cup sugar
> 3 teaspoons baking powder
> 1/2 teaspoon salt

6 Gently stir in ▬ ▬ ▬ ▬ ▬ ▬ ▬ ➤

> **1 cup fresh or drained canned blueberries or 3/4 cup frozen blueberries, thawed and well drained**

7 Spoon batter into muffin cups until 2/3 full. Sprinkle each with about 2 teaspoons of topping mixture.

8 Bake 20 to 25 minutes or until golden brown. **Adult help:** Immediately remove muffins from pan to wire rack. Serve warm or cool.

Here's another idea. . . Make **Apple Muffins**: Leave out blueberries. Stir in 1 cup grated apple with the milk, and stir in 1/2 teaspoon ground cinnamon with the flour in step 5. Bake 25 to 30 minutes.

Nutrition Per Muffin: Calories 195 (Calories from Fat 70); Fat 8g (Saturated 1g); Cholesterol 20mg; Sodium 250mg; Carbohydrate 29g (Dietary Fiber 1g); Protein 3g

Amanda liked the ease of this recipe and says they can be mixed up in about 10 to 15 minutes and baked in 20 minutes. That's fast!

CINNAMON-SUGAR
▲▲▲▲▲ MUFFINS ▲▲▲▲▲

12 Muffins

Utensils You Will Need

Muffin pan with medium cups, 2 1/2 × 1 1/4 inches • Pastry brush •
Medium bowl • Fork • Dry-ingredient measuring cups • Wooden spoon •
Small bowl • Measuring spoons • Liquid measuring cup • Pot holders •
1-quart saucepan

1 Heat oven to 350°.

2 Grease bottoms only of 12 muffin
cups with ▬ ▬ ▬ ▬ ▬ ▬ ▬ ▬ ▶

> **Shortening**

3 Beat in medium bowl with fork ▬ ▬ ▶

> **1/2 cup sugar**
> **1/2 cup milk**
> **1/3 cup vegetable oil**
> **1 large egg**

4 Stir into milk mixture just until all
the flour is wet (do not stir too
much—batter will be lumpy) ▬ ▬ ▬ ▶

> **1 1/2 cups all-purpose flour**
> **1 1/2 teaspoons baking powder**
> **1/2 teaspoon salt**
> **1/4 teaspoon ground nutmeg**

5 Spoon batter into muffin cups until
2/3 full. Bake 20 to 25 minutes or
until golden brown.

6 While muffins are baking, mix in
small bowl, then set aside ▬ ▬ ▬ ▬ ▶

> **1/2 cup sugar**
> **1 teaspoon ground cinnamon**

7 Melt in saucepan over low heat, then
remove from heat ▬ ▬ ▬ ▬ ▬ ▬ ▶

> **1/2 cup (1 stick) margarine or
> butter**

8 **Adult help:** Immediately remove
muffins from pan. Roll hot muffins in the melted margarine, then in the
cinnamon-sugar mixture. Serve hot.

Nutrition Per Muffin: *Calories 260 (Calories from Fat 135); Fat 15g (Saturated 3g); Cholesterol 19mg;*
Sodium 250mg; Carbohydrate 30g (Dietary Fiber 0g); Protein 3g

Cinnamon-Sugar Muffins, Butter-dipped Biscuit Sticks (page 108)

GINGERBREAD MUFFINS WITH
ORANGE SPREAD

15 muffins

Utensils You Will Need

Muffin pan with medium cups, 2 1/2 × 1 1/4 inches • Large bowl •
Liquid measuring cup • Electric mixer • Toothpick • Pot holders •
Wire cooling rack • Small bowl • Dry-ingredient measuring cups • Grater •
Measuring spoons

1 Heat oven to 400°. Line 15 muffin cups with paper baking cups.

2 Beat in large bowl with electric mixer
on low speed about 1 minute or until
slightly thickened – – – – – – – ➤

> **1 package (14.5 ounces) ginger-
> bread cake and cookie mix
> 1 cup lukewarm water
> 1 large egg**

3 Spoon batter into muffin cups until
about 2/3 full. Bake 16 to 18 minutes
or until toothpick poked in center
comes out clean.

4 While muffins are baking, beat in
small bowl with electric mixer on
low speed about 15 seconds or
until mixed – – – – – – – ➤

> **1 cup powdered sugar
> 1/2 cup (1 stick) margarine or
> butter, softened
> 1 teaspoon grated orange peel
> 1 tablespoon orange juice**

5 Beat orange mixture with electric
mixer on high speed about 2 minutes
or until fluffy. Cover with plastic
wrap and refrigerate until
serving time.

6 **Adult help:** Immediately remove muffins from pan to wire rack. Serve
warm or cool with orange spread.

Nutrition Per Muffin: Calories 215 (Calories from Fat 90); Fat 10g (Saturated 2g); Cholesterol 15mg; Sodium 270mg; Carbohydrate 29g (Dietary Fiber 0g); Protein 2g

Persis thought these muffins were fun and easy to make and tasted so good that she served them to her family for dessert!

▲▲▲▲▲ ELEPHANT EARS ▲▲▲▲▲

4 servings

Utensils You Will Need

Cookie sheet • Pastry brush • 1-quart saucepan • Small sharp knife •
Medium bowl • Dry-ingredient measuring cups • Measuring spoons •
Wooden spoon • Liquid measuring cup • Rolling pin • Ruler • Small bowl •
Sharp knife • Pot holders • Spatula • Wire cooling rack

1 Heat oven to 425°.

2 Grease cookie sheet with - - - ➤ | **Shortening**

3 Melt in saucepan over low heat, then set aside - - - - - ➤ | **1/4 cup (1/2 stick) margarine or butter**

4 Mix in medium bowl with wooden spoon - - - - - ➤ | **1 cup all-purpose flour**
2 tablespoons sugar
1/2 teaspoon baking powder
1/2 teaspoon salt

5 Stir in to make a dough - - - ➤ | **3 tablespoons of the melted margarine or butter**
1/3 cup milk

6 Sprinkle a clean surface (such as a kitchen counter or breadboard) with flour. Put dough on surface. Roll ball of dough around 3 or 4 times. Knead dough quickly and lightly by folding, pressing and turning. Repeat 10 times. Roll or pat dough into 9 × 5-inch rectangle.

7 Mix in small bowl - - - - - ➤ | **2 tablespoons sugar**
1 teaspoon ground cinnamon

8 Brush dough with the rest of the melted margarine or butter, then sprinkle with the sugar-cinnamon mixture.

9 Roll dough up tightly, beginning at short end of rectangle. Pinch edge of dough into roll to seal. **Adult help:** Cut roll into 4 equal pieces with sharp knife. Put pieces, cut sides up, on cookie sheet, then pat into 6-inch circles.

10 Sprinkle circles with ▬ ▬ ▬ ▬ ▬ ➤

Sugar

11 Bake 8 to 10 minutes or until edges are golden brown. Immediately remove elephant ears from cookie sheet with spatula to wire rack. Cool.

Nutrition Per Elephant Ear: Calories 375 (Calories from Fat 190); Fat 21g (Saturated 4g); Cholesterol 5mg; Sodium 570mg; Carbohydrate 44g (Dietary Fiber 1g); Protein 4g

HINT
Dip hands in sugar to keep them from sticking to dough when patting circles on cookie sheet.

BUTTER-DIPPED
▲▲▲▲▲ BISCUIT STICKS ▲▲▲▲▲

16 servings

Utensils You Will Need

Square pan, 9 × 9 × 2 inches • Small sharp knife • Pot holders • Medium bowl • Dry-ingredient measuring cups • Measuring spoons • Wooden spoon • Fork • Liquid measuring cup • Rolling pin • Ruler • Sharp knife

1 Heat oven to 450°.

2 **Adult help:** Melt in square pan in oven, then remove pan from oven ➡

> **1/4 cup (1/2 stick) margarine or butter**

3 Mix in medium bowl with wooden spoon ➡

> **1 1/3 cups all-purpose flour**
> **2 teaspoons sugar**
> **2 teaspoons baking powder**
> **1 teaspoon salt**

4 Stir in with fork about 30 strokes to make a dough ➡

> **2/3 cup milk**

5 Sprinkle a clean surface (such as a kitchen counter or breadboard) with flour. Put dough on surface. Roll ball of dough around 3 or 4 times. Knead dough quickly and lightly by folding, pressing and turning. Repeat 10 times.

6 Roll or pat dough into 8-inch square. **Adult help:** Cut dough in half with knife dipped in flour, then cut each half crosswise into 8 strips.

7 Dip each strip in the melted margarine in the pan, coating both sides. Put strips close together in 2 rows in pan.

8 Bake 15 to 20 minutes or until golden brown.

Here's another idea. . . Make **Seasoned Butter-dipped Sticks**: Make recipe for Butter-dipped Biscuit Sticks (above)—except sprinkle strips with caraway, celery, poppy or sesame seed, dried oregano leaves or garlic salt after coating with margarine.

Nutrition Per Biscuit: Calories 70 (Calories from Fat 25); Fat 3g (Saturated 1g); Cholesterol 6mg; Sodium 235mg; Carbohydrate 9g (Dietary Fiber 0g); Protein 1g

HINT
a pizza cutter makes quick work of cutting the dough into strips.

Justin thought these biscuits were really easy to make and would go great with spaghetti, soup or chili or to take on picnics.

▲▲▲▲ SCONES ▲▲▲▲

8 scones

Utensils You Will Need

Cookie sheet • Pastry brush • Medium bowl • Wooden spoon •
Dry-ingredient measuring cup • Liquid measuring cup • Measuring spoons •
Ruler • Sharp knife • Pot holders • Spatula • Wire cooling rack

1 Heat oven to 425°.

2 Grease cookie sheet with – – – – → | **Shortening** |

3 Mix in medium bowl with wooden
spoon to make a dough – – – – → | **2 cups Bisquick® Original baking mix**
1/3 cup milk
3 tablespoons sugar
1 large egg |

4 Sprinkle a clean surface (such as a
kitchen counter or breadboard)
with flour. Put dough on surface.
Roll ball of dough around 3 or
4 times. Knead dough quickly and
lightly by folding, pressing and turning. Repeat 10 times.

5 Pat dough into 8-inch circle on cookie sheet. (If dough is sticky, dip your
fingers in flour or baking mix before patting.)

6 Brush dough lightly, using pastry
brush, with – – – – → | **Milk** |

7 Sprinkle dough with – – – – → | **1/2 teaspoon sugar** |

8 **Adult help:** Cut dough into 8 wedges.
(Leave wedges in circle.) Bake about 12 minutes or until golden brown.
Carefully break wedges apart with spatula, then remove to wire rack. Serve
warm.

Nutrition Per Scone: 155 Calories (Calories from Fat 45); Fat 5g (Saturated 1g); Cholesterol 30mg; Sodium 440mg; Carbohydrate 24g (Dietary Fiber 0g); Protein 3g

▲▲▲▲▲ BUTTONS AND BOWS ▲▲▲▲▲

About 8 buttons and bows

Utensils You Will Need

Medium bowl • Dry-ingredient measuring cups • Measuring spoons •
Liquid measuring cup • Wooden spoon • Rolling pin • Ruler •
Doughnut cutter • Cookie sheet • Spatula • Pot holders • 1-quart saucepan •
Wire cooling rack • Small bowl

1 Heat oven to 400°.

2 Mix in medium bowl with wooden
spoon to make a soft dough ➤

> **2 cups Bisquick® Original
> baking mix
> 1/3 cup milk
> 2 tablespoons sugar
> 1 teaspoon ground nutmeg
> 1/8 teaspoon ground cinnamon
> 1 large egg**

3 Sprinkle a clean surface (such as a
kitchen counter or breadboard)
with flour. Put dough on surface.
Roll ball of dough around 3 or
4 times. Knead dough quickly and
lightly by folding, pressing and
turning. Repeat 5 times.

4 Roll or pat dough until 1/2 inch thick. Cut dough with doughnut cutter
dipped in flour. To make bow shapes, hold opposite sides of each ring of
dough, then twist to make a figure 8. Put bows and buttons (the dough
from the center of each ring) on cookie sheet.

5 Bake 8 to 10 minutes or until light brown.

6 While buttons and bows are baking,
melt in saucepan over low heat ➤

> **1/4 cup (1/2 stick) margarine
> or butter**

7 Put in a small bowl ━ ━ ━ ━ ━ ━ ➤ | 1/2 cup sugar

8 **Adult help:** Remove buttons and bows
from cookie sheet with spatula to wire rack. Immediately dip each button
and bow in the melted margarine, then in the sugar. Serve warm.

Nutrition Per Button and Bow: Calories 250 (Calories from Fat 100); Fat 11g (Saturated 3g); Cholesterol 30mg; Sodium 510mg; Carbohydrate 35g (Dietary Fiber 0g); Protein 3g

Cory had fun cutting the buttons and bows and served them on the fanciest plate he could find!

▲▲▲▲ SNOWMAN BUNS ▲▲▲▲

12 buns

Utensils You Will Need

Large bowl • Kitchen scissors • Liquid measuring cup • Wooden spoon •
Dry-ingredient measuring cups • Measuring spoons • Electric mixer •
Kitchen towel • Cookie sheet • Pastry brush • Pot holders • Spatula •
Wire cooling rack

1 Pour into large bowl ▪ ▪ ▪ ▪ ▪ ▪ ▶ | **3/4 cup warm water**

2 Sprinkle over warm water, then let
stand a few minutes to soften ▪ ▪ ▪ ▶ | **1 package regular or
quick-acting active dry yeast**

3 Add to yeast mixture, then beat
with electric mixer on low speed
30 seconds, scraping bowl all
the time ▪ ▪ ▪ ▪ ▪ ▪ ▪ ▪ ▪ ▶ | **1/3 cup sugar
1/4 cup shortening
1 teaspoon salt
1 teaspoon ground nutmeg
2 large eggs
2 cups all-purpose flour**

4 Beat dough with electric mixer on
medium speed 2 minutes, scraping
bowl a few times.

5 Stir in until smooth ▪ ▪ ▪ ▪ ▪ ▶ | **1 1/2 cups all-purpose flour**

6 Cover dough with towel and let rise
in warm place about 45 minutes or until dough doubles. (Dough is ready if
a mark stays when dough is touched.)

7 Grease cookie sheet with ▪ ▪ ▪ ▪ ▶ | **Shortening**

8 Stir down dough by beating
25 strokes with wooden spoon. Sprinkle a clean surface (such as a kitchen
counter or breadboard) with flour. Put dough on surface. Gently roll dough
in flour to coat. **Adult help:** Cut dough into 12 equal pieces with sharp
knife.

9 To shape each snowman: Shape half of each dough piece into 4-inch oval for the body. Shape half of the rest of the dough piece into a ball for the head and attach it to the body. Press in a tiny piece of dough for the nose. Shape rest of dough piece into 4-inch roll. Cut roll in half, and attach pieces to body for arms.

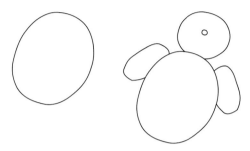

10 Arrange snowmen about 3 inches apart on cookie sheet. Cover snowmen with towel and let rise in warm place about 45 minutes or until snowmen double.

11 Heat oven to 350°.

12 For each snowman, press in 2 for eyes and 3 for buttons from ▬ ▬ ▬ ▬ ▬ ▬ ➤

> **60 currants**
> **(about 1 1/2 teaspoons)**

13 Beat in small bowl with fork, then brush on snowmen ▬ ▬ ▬ ▬ ▬ ▬ ▬ ➤

> **1 large egg**

14 Bake about 15 minutes or until golden brown. **Adult help:** Remove from cookie sheet with spatula to wire rack. Serve warm.

Here's another idea. . . Make **Snowflakes:** Cut dough into 24 equal pieces. Shape each piece into a ball. Put 4 balls with sides touching in the shape of a square on cookie sheet greased with shortening. Repeat with remaining balls to make 6 squares. Cover and let rise in warm place about 45 minutes or until squares double. Prepare Baked-on Frosting (page 43). Outline snowflake designs on each bun with frosting. Bake 12 to 15 minutes. 2 dozen buns.

Nutrition Per Bun: Calories 230 (Calories from Fat 55); Fat 6g (Saturated 2g); Cholesterol 55mg; Sodium 200mg; Carbohydrate 39g (Dietary Fiber 1g); Protein 6g

▲▲▲▲▲ CHEESY PRETZELS ▲▲▲▲▲

16 pretzels

Utensils You Will Need

Cookie sheet • Pastry brush • Medium bowl • Fork •
Dry-ingredient measuring cups • Liquid measuring cup • Measuring spoons •
Rolling pin • Ruler • Knife • Small bowl • Pot holders • Spatula •
Wire cooling rack

1 Heat oven to 400°.

2 Generously grease cookie sheet
with ⇢

> **Shortening**

3 Mix in medium bowl with fork to
make a dough ⇢

> **1 1/2 cups all-purpose flour**
> **1/2 cup shredded Cheddar**
> **cheese (2 ounces)**
> **2/3 cup milk**
> **2 tablespoons (from a stick)**
> **margarine or butter**
> **2 teaspoons baking powder**
> **1 teaspoon sugar**
> **1/2 teaspoon salt**

4 Sprinkle a clean surface (such as a
kitchen counter or breadboard) with
flour. Put dough on surface. Roll
ball of dough around 3 or 4 times.
Knead dough quickly and lightly
by folding, pressing and turning.
Repeat 10 times.

5 Divide dough in half. Roll or pat
half of the dough into 12 × 8-inch
rectangle. **Adult help:** Cut dough lengthwise into eight 1-inch-wide strips.
Fold each strip lengthwise in half to make it more narrow. Pinch the edges
to seal.

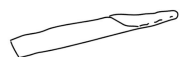

6 Twist each strip into a pretzel shape. Put pretzels, seam sides down, on cookie sheet.

7 Beat in small bowl with fork = = = ➤ | **1 large egg** |

8 Brush pretzels with the beaten egg, then sprinkle lightly with = = = = ➤ | **Coarse salt** |

9 Bake 10 to 15 minutes or until golden brown. Remove pretzels from cookie sheet with spatula to wire rack. Cool. Repeat making pretzels with the rest of the dough.

Here's another idea. . . Make **Peanutty Pretzels:** Leave out the cheese. Use 2 tablespoons crunchy peanut butter in place of the margarine. Use 2 tablespoons chopped salted peanuts in place of the coarse salt.

Nutrition Per Pretzel: Calories 80 (Calories from Fat 25); Fat 3g (Saturated 1g); Cholesterol 20mg; Sodium 580mg; Carbohydrate 10g (Dietary Fiber 0g); Protein 3g

HINT
A pizza cutter makes quick work of cutting the dough into strips.

5

Fantastic Desserts, Pies and Crisps

Sugar Cookie Tarts (page 128)

STRAWBERRY PIE ▲▲▲▲▲

8 servings

Utensils You Will Need

2 medium bowls • Dry-ingredient measuring cups • Measuring spoons • Fork •
Pastry blender • Pastry cloth and cloth cover for rolling pin • Rolling pin •
Pie plate, 9 × 1 1/2 inches • Colander • Sharp knife • Potato masher •
Pot holders • Wire cooling rack • 1 1/2-quart saucepan •
Liquid measuring cup • Wooden spoon

1 Heat oven to 475°.

2 Mix in medium bowl with fork ➤

> **1 cup all-purpose flour**
> **1/2 teaspoon salt**

3 Cut into flour mixture with pastry blender until pieces are the size of small peas ➤

> **1/3 cup plus 1 tablespoon shortening**

4 Sprinkle in, 1 tablespoon at a time, tossing with fork until all the flour is wet and pastry almost leaves side of bowl ➤

> **2 to 3 tablespoons cold water**

5 Cover a breadboard with a pastry cloth. Sprinkle flour lightly over cloth. Shape pastry into a ball on floured cloth. Shape ball into a flattened round. Roll pastry with floured cloth-covered rolling pin until pastry is 2 inches larger than pie plate turned upside down.

6 Fold pastry into fourths. Put pastry in pie plate. Unfold and fit pastry into plate, pressing firmly against bottom and side. Trim edge of pastry that hangs over pie plate to 1 inch from rim of plate. Fold and roll pastry under, even with pie plate, then press around edge with fork dipped in flour. Poke bottom and side of pastry many times with fork.

7 Bake 8 to 10 minutes or until crust is light brown. Cool completely on wire rack.

8 Wash in colander, then remove stems from ▪ ▪ ▪ ▪ ▪ ▪ ▪ ▪ ▪ ➤ **6 cups whole strawberries**

9 Mash 2 cups of the strawberries in medium bowl with potato masher or fork to measure 1 cup mashed strawberries. Save the rest of the strawberries for step #14.

10 Mix in saucepan with wooden spoon ▪ ▪ ▪ ▪ ▪ ▪ ▪ ▪ ▪ ➤ **1 cup sugar**
2 tablespoons cornstarch

11 Stir in ▪ ▪ ▪ ▪ ▪ ▪ ▪ ▪ ▪ ➤ **The mashed strawberries**
1/2 cup water

12 **Adult help:** Cook sugar-strawberry mixture over medium-high heat, stirring all the time, until mixture thickens and boils. Boil and stir 1 minute, then cool.

13 Beat until smooth with wooden spoon, then spread over bottom of pie crust ▪ ▪ ▪ ▪ ▪ ▪ ▪ ▪ ▪ ➤ **1 package (3 ounces) cream cheese, softened**

14 Pile whole strawberries on cream cheese in pie crust. Pour cooked strawberry mixture over top. Refrigerate about 2 hours or until set. Cover and refrigerate any leftover pie.

Here's another idea. . . Make **Raspberry Pie**: Use 6 cups raspberries in place of the strawberries.

Nutrition Per Serving: *Calories 320 (Calories from Fat 125); Fat 14g (Saturated 5g); Cholesterol 10mg; Sodium 170mg; Carbohydrate 47g (Dietary Fiber 2g); Protein 3g*

LEMON-CREAM CHEESE ▲▲▲▲▲ DESSERT ▲▲▲▲▲

9 servings

Utensils You Will Need

Plastic bag with zipper top • Dry-ingredient measuring cups • Rolling pin •
Small bowl • Measuring spoons • Wooden spoon •
Square pan, 8 × 8 × 2 inches • Wire cooling rack • Large bowl •
Electric mixer • Can opener • Liquid measuring cup • Plastic wrap

1 Heat oven to 350°.

2 Put in plastic bag - - - - - - - → | **3 cups toasted whole-grain oat cereal**

3 Press air out of plastic bag, then seal. Roll cereal with rolling pin or jar until finely crushed.

4 Mix in small bowl with wooden spoon, then save 2 tablespoons - - → | **The crushed cereal**
1/3 cup (from a stick) margarine or butter, melted
1/4 cup sugar
1 teaspoon ground cinnamon

5 Press the rest of the cereal mixture in square pan. Bake 12 minutes. Cool on wire rack.

6 Beat in large bowl with electric mixer on medium speed until light and fluffy - - - - - - - → | **1 package (8 ounces) cream cheese, softened**

7 Beat in, a little at a time - - - - → | **1 can (14 ounces) sweetened condensed milk**

8 Stir in - - - - - - - - → | **1/4 cup lemon juice**
1 teaspoon vanilla

9 Pour cream cheese mixture over baked cereal mixture in pan. Sprinkle saved cereal mixture over top. Cover with plastic wrap and refrigerate 3 to 4 hours or until firm.

10 If you like, top with ▬ ▬ ▬ ▬ ▬ ➤ **Fresh fruit**

11 Cover and refrigerate any leftover dessert.

Nutrition Per Serving: Calories 325 (Calories from Fat 180); Fat 20g (Saturated 9g); Cholesterol 45mg; Sodium 290mg; Carbohydrate 31g (Dietary Fiber 1g); Protein 6g

Sara liked crunching up the cereal and using the mixer to make this delightful dish so much, that she prefers to call it Crunchy Cheese Cake.

STRAWBERRY
▲▲▲▲▲ SHORTCAKES ▲▲▲▲▲

6 shortcakes

Utensils You Will Need

Colander • Small sharp knife • Paper towel • Cutting board • Medium bowl •
Wooden spoon • Dry-ingredient measuring cups • Large bowl •
Liquid measuring cup • Measuring spoons • Rolling pin • Ruler •
3-inch round cookie cutter • Cookie sheet • Pot holders • Spatula •
Wire cooling rack • Spoon

1 Rinse in colander ▬ ▬ ▬ ▬ ▬ ▬ ➤ | **1 quart whole strawberries**

2 Gently pat strawberries dry with paper towel. Remove stems from strawberries. **Adult help:** Cut strawberries in half. Put strawberries in medium bowl.

3 Stir in, then cover and refrigerate ▬ ➤ | **1/2 cup sugar**

4 Heat oven to 425°.

5 Mix in large bowl with wooden spoon to make a soft dough ▬ ▬ ▬ ➤

> **2 1/3 cups Bisquick® Original baking mix**
> **1/2 cup half-and-half**
> **3 tablespoons sugar**
> **3 tablespoons (from a stick) margarine or butter, melted**

6 Sprinkle a clean surface (such as a kitchen counter or breadboard) with flour or baking mix. Put dough on surface. Roll ball of dough around 3 or 4 times. Knead dough quickly and lightly by folding, pressing and turning. Repeat 10 times.

7 Roll or pat dough until 1/2 inch thick. Cut dough with cookie cutter dipped in flour. Carefully put dough on cookie sheet.

8 Bake 12 to 15 minutes or until golden brown.

9 While shortcakes are baking, make ‐ ‐ ‐ ‐ ‐ ‐ ‐ ‐ ‐ ‐ ‐ ▶

> **Sweetened Whipped Cream (page 65)**

10 **Adult help:** Remove shortcakes from cookie sheet with spatula to wire rack. Split shortcakes horizontally in half with knife, then put on dessert plates. Spoon strawberries between shortcake halves and over tops. Top with the whipped cream.

Nutrition Per Shortcake: Calories 485 (Calories from Fat 215); Fat 24g (Saturated 10g); Cholesterol 40mg; Sodium 750mg; Carbohydrate 64g (Dietary Fiber 2g); Protein 5g

HINT
Cut 3 nicely shaped strawberreis with green tops in half lengthwise and use to top shortcakes.

MINI PINE-APPLE ▲▲▲▲▲ DESSERTS ▲▲▲▲▲

6 servings

Utensils You Will Need

Pie plate, 9 × 1 1/2 inches • Fork • Dry-ingredient measuring cups •
Measuring spoons • Small sharp knife • Pot holders • 1 1/2-quart saucepan •
Can opener • Grater • Six 6-ounce custard cups

1 Heat oven to 400°.

2 Mix in pie plate with fork until
crumbly ▶

> 1/2 cup Bisquick® Original
> baking mix
> 3 tablespoons sugar
> 2 tablespoons finely chopped
> nuts
> 2 tablespoons (from a stick)
> margarine or butter, softened
> 1/4 teaspoon ground cinnamon

3 Bake 8 to 10 minutes or until light and
dry. Stir with fork.

4 Heat in saucepan, stirring a few times,
until hot ▶

> 1 can (21 ounces) apple pie
> filling
> 1 can (8.25 ounces) crushed
> pineapple in syrup, undrained
> 1 teaspoon grated orange peel

5 Spoon apple mixture into custard cups.
Sprinkle with baked topping. Store any
leftover topping in tightly covered container in refrigerator.

Nutrition Per Serving: Calories 260 (Calories from Fat 80); Fat 9g
(Saturated 2g); Cholesterol 0mg; Sodium 210mg; Carbohydrate 46g
(Dietary Fiber 2g); Protein 1g

**Mike thought these mini treats were super easy to
make and that they would also be good made with
cherry or strawberry pie filling. He suggested
putting whipped cream on top—an idea we like!**

Strawberry Shortcakes (page 124)

▲▲▲▲▲ SUGAR COOKIE TARTS ▲▲▲▲▲

30 cookies *(photo page 119)*

Utensils You Will Need

Large bowl • Dry-ingredient measuring cups • Small sharp knife •
Measuring spoons • Wooden spoon • Rolling pin • Ruler •
3-inch round cookie cutter • Cookie sheet • Pot holders • Spatula •
Wire cooling rack • Small bowl • Knife • Teaspoon

1 Heat oven to 375°.

2 Mix in large bowl with wooden
spoon ➡

> **2 cups sugar**
> **1 cup shortening**
> **3/4 cup (1 1/2 sticks) mar-
> garine or butter, softened**
> **2 teaspoons vanilla**
> **1 large egg**

3 Stir in ➡

> **3 1/2 cups all-purpose flour**
> **1 teaspoon baking powder**
> **1/4 teaspoon salt**

4 Sprinkle a clean surface (such as a
kitchen counter or breadboard)
with flour. Put dough on surface.
Divide dough in half. Roll half of dough at a time until 1/4 inch thick. Cut
dough with cookie cutter dipped in flour. Put cookies 2 inches apart on
cookie sheet.

5 Bake 10 to 12 minutes or until light brown. Cool cookies on cookie sheet
1 minute, then remove with spatula to wire rack. Cool completely.

6 Mix in small bowl with wooden
until smooth ➡

> **1 package (8 ounces) cream
> cheese, softened**
> **1/2 cup sugar**
> **1 teaspoon vanilla**

7 Spread about 2 teaspoons cream cheese
mixture over each cookie.

8 Arrange on cookies ▬ ▬ ▬ ▬ ▬ ▬ ➤ **Toppings (sliced fresh fruit, miniature semisweet chocolate chips, chopped nuts or jam with toasted sliced almonds)**

9 Cover and refrigerate any leftover tarts.

Nutrition Per Cookie: Calories 250 (Calories from Fat 125); Fat 14g (Saturated 4g); Cholesterol 15mg; Sodium 110mg; Carbohydrate 30g (Dietary Fiber 1g); Protein 2g

HINT
Dip banana slices in a little lemon juice so they won't turn brown.

▲▲▲▲▲ YUMMY YOGURT CUPS ▲▲▲▲▲

4 servings

♀♀♀ Utensils You Will Need

Medium bowl • Dry-ingredient measuring cups • Small sharp knife •
Measuring spoons • Fork • Tablespoon • Four 6-ounce custard cups •
Pot holders • Small metal spatula • Wire cooling rack • Spoon

1 Heat oven to 375°.

2 Mix in medium bowl with fork
until crumbly ▬ ▬ ▬ ▬ ▬ ▬ ▬ ➤

> **3/4 cup all-purpose flour**
> **1/4 cup (1/2 stick) margarine**
> **or butter, softened**
> **3 tablespoons powdered sugar**

3 Sprinkle in, 1 teaspoon at a time,
stirring to make a dough ▬ ▬ ▬ ▬ ➤

> **2 to 3 teaspoons cold water**

4 Press about 3 tablespoons of the
dough in bottom and up side of each custard cup to within 1/2 inch of top.

5 Bake 10 to 12 minutes or until golden brown. Cool 10 minutes. **Adult
help:** Carefully remove shells from custard cups with small metal spatula to
wire rack. Cool completely.

6 Spoon evenly into shells ▬ ▬ ▬ ▬ ➤

> **1 1/3 cups yogurt (any flavor)**

7 If you like, top with ▬ ▬ ▬ ▬ ▬ ➤

> **Fresh fruit**

*Nutrition Per Serving: Calories 295 (Calories from Fat 115); Fat 13g (Saturated 3g); Cholesterol 5mg;
Sodium 180mg; Carbohydrate 39g (Dietary Fiber 1g); Protein 6g*

Persis thought it was neat that you eat your dish. She also suggests topping them with crumbled candy, cookies or granola bars, and that we add "yummy" to the title.

HINT
Keep edges of dough even when pressing it into custard cups.

▲▲▲▲▲ EASY PUMPKIN-NUT PIE ▲▲▲▲▲

8 servings

Utensils You Will Need

2 large bowls • Dry-ingredient measuring cups • Wooden spoons •
Measuring spoons • Pie plate, 9 × 1 1/2 inches • Fork • Can opener •
Aluminum foil • Pot holders • Knife • Wire cooling rack • Medium bowl •
Liquid measuring cup • Eggbeater

1 Mix in large bowl with wooden spoon ‑ ‑ ‑ ‑ ‑ ‑ ‑ ‑ ‑ ➤

> 1/2 cup (1 stick) margarine or butter, softened
> 1/3 cup packed brown sugar

2 Stir in just until crumbly ‑ ‑ ‑ ‑ ‑ ➤

3 Press mixture against bottom and up side of pie plate, building up a 1/2-inch edge above top of pie plate. (A high edge is necessary to keep filling from running over.)

> 1 1/4 cups all-purpose or whole wheat flour
> 1/2 cup chopped nuts
> 1/2 teaspoon vanilla
> 1/4 teaspoon salt
> 1/4 teaspoon baking soda

4 Heat oven to 425°.

5 Beat slightly in large bowl with fork ‑ ‑ ‑ ‑ ‑ ‑ ‑ ‑ ➤

> 2 large eggs

6 Stir in until smooth ‑ ‑ ‑ ‑ ‑ ‑ ➤

> 1 cup mashed pumpkin (about half of a 16-ounce can)
> 3/4 cup packed brown sugar
> 1 teaspoon ground cinnamon
> 1/2 teaspoon salt
> 1/4 teaspoon ground cloves
> 1/4 teaspoon ground ginger
> 1/4 teaspoon ground nutmeg

7 Stir in, a little at a time ▬ ▬ ▬ ▬ ▬ ➤

> **1 can (12 ounces) evaporated milk**

8 Pour pumpkin mixture into pie crust. Cover edge of crust with 2- to 3-inch strip of aluminum foil to keep crust from browning too much.

9 Bake 15 minutes. Turn oven temperature down to 350°. Bake 45 to 55 minutes longer or until knife poked in pie near center comes out clean. Cool completely on wire rack.

10 Chill medium bowl in freezer about 15 minutes or until cold.

11 Beat in chilled bowl with eggbeater until stiff ▬ ▬ ▬ ▬ ▬ ▬ ▬ ➤

> **1 cup whipping (heavy) cream**
> **3 tablespoons packed brown sugar**

12 Serve pie with the whipped cream. Cover and refrigerate any leftover pie and whipped cream.

Nutrition Per Serving: Calories 540 (Calories from Fat 270); Fat 30g (Saturated 11g); Cholesterol 100mg; Sodium 460mg; Carbohydrate 59g (Dietary Fiber 1g); Protein 9g

Kirsten thought the pie was fun to make—her mom sat at the table while *she* did the baking!

EASY FUN DOUGH

Mix up your own fun dough to keep on hand for whenever the urge to create strikes. Try using different gadgets like pinking shears, cookie cutters, a garlic press or pizza roller to make designs and shapes. You can even turn them into decorations. Be creative!

1 Mix in microwavable 4-cup measuring cup ▪ ▪ ▪ ▪ ▪ ▪ ▪ ▶

> **1 1/4 cups Bisquick® Original baking mix**
> **1/4 cup salt**
> **1 teaspoon cream of tartar**

2 Mix in liquid measuring cup ▪ ▪ ▪ ▶

> **1 cup water**
> **1 teaspoon food color**

3 Stir the colored water into the dry mixture, a little at a time, until all the liquid is added. Microwave uncovered on High (100%) 1 minute. Scrape the mixture from the side of the cup and stir.

4 Microwave uncovered 2 to 3 minutes longer, stirring every minute, until the mixture forms sort of a ball. Let the dough stand uncovered about 3 minutes.

5 Use the spoon to take the dough out of the measuring cup. Knead dough in your hands or on the counter about 1 minute or until smooth. (If the dough is sticky, add 1 to 2 tablespoons of Bisquick®.) Cool about 15 minutes or until cool enough to handle. Store in Refrigerator in plastic bag.

Easy Fun Dough can also be baked like cookie dough. Just follow these directions:

1 Heat oven to 225°. Roll dough about 1/8 inch thick. Cut out desired shapes with cookie cutters, or shape the dough into whatever you want. Make a hole in the top of each ornament using the end of a plastic straw. Place on ungreased cookie sheet.

2 Bake 1 hour. **Adult help:** Turn the ornaments over. Bake 1 to 1 1/2 hours longer or until ornaments sound brittle when tapped.

3 Remove ornaments from cookie sheet with spatula to wire rack. Cool completely. Tie ribbon or yarn through the holes.

QUICK BLUEBERRY ▲▲▲▲▲ COBBLER ▲▲▲▲▲

6 servings

Utensils You Will Need

1 1/2-quart casserole • Can opener • Wooden spoon • Small bowl •
Dry-ingredient measuring cup • Measuring spoons • Liquid measuring cup •
Small sharp knife • Tablespoon • Pot holders • Wire cooling rack

1 Heat oven to 400°.

2 Mix in casserole with wooden spoon ▬ ▬ ▬ ▬ ▬ ▬ ▬ ▬ ▶

> **1 can (21 ounces) blueberry pie filling**
> **1 teaspoon grated orange peel, if you like**

3 Bake uncovered about 15 minutes or until hot and bubbly.

4 While blueberry mixture is baking, stir in small bowl to make a soft dough ▬ ▬ ▬ ▬ ▬ ▬ ▬ ▶

> **1 cup Bisquick® Original baking mix**
> **1 tablespoon sugar**
> **1/4 cup orange juice**
> **1 tablespoon (from a stick) margarine or butter, softened**

5 **Adult help:** Drop dough by 6 spoonfuls onto hot blueberry mixture. Bake uncovered 20 to 25 minutes or until topping is light brown. Cool slightly on wire rack. Serve warm.

Here's another idea. . . Make **Quick Cherry-Almond Cobbler**: Use 1 can (21 ounces) cherry pie filling in place of the blueberry pie filling, 1/2 teaspoon almond extract in place of the orange peel and 1/4 cup milk in place of the orange juice. Stir 2 tablespoons toasted slivered almonds into the dough in step 4.

Nutrition Per Serving: *Calories 235 (Calories from Fat 65); Fat 7g (Saturated 2g); Cholesterol 0mg; Sodium 330mg; Carbohydrate 43g (Dietary Fiber 2g); Protein 2g*

Quick Blueberry Cobbler

▲▲▲▲▲ APPLE CRISP ▲▲▲▲▲

4 servings

Utensils You Will Need

Square pan, 8 × 8 × 2 inches • Cutting board • Sharp knives •
Dry-ingredient measuring cups • Small bowl • Measuring spoons •
Liquid measuring cup • Medium bowl • Pot holders • Wire cooling rack

1 Heat oven to 375°.

2 **Adult help:** Cut into fourths, then core, peel and slice to measure 4 cups - - - - - - - - - - - - - - ▶ | **About 5 medium cooking apples**

3 Put apple slices in square pan.

4 Mix in small bowl, then sprinkle over apples - - - - - - - - - - - ▶ | **1/4 cup granulated or packed brown sugar**
1/2 teaspoon ground cinnamon

5 Pour over apples - - - - - - - - ▶ | **1/4 cup water**

6 Mix with hands in medium bowl until crumbly, then sprinkle over apples - - - - - - - - - - ▶ | **1 cup all-purpose flour**
2/3 cup granulated sugar
1/2 cup (1 stick) margarine or butter, softened

7 Bake 45 to 50 minutes or until apples are tender and topping is golden brown. Cool on wire rack.

8 If you like, serve with - - - - - ▶ | **Sweetened Whipped Cream (page 65) or ice cream**

Nutrition Per Serving: *Calories 590 (Calories from Fat 215);*
Fat 24g (Saturated 5g); Cholesterol 0mg; Sodium 270mg;
Carbohydrate 94g (Dietary Fiber 4g); Protein 3g

HINT
*You can leave
the peel on the
apples, if you
like.*

**Cory liked making this recipe because he enjoyed
peeling the apples—his mom liked it because it uses
ingredients she had on hand, and she didn't have
to make a special trip to the store. Cory served the
crisp topped with ice cream and butterscotch
topping. Yum!**

METRIC CONVERSION GUIDE

VOLUME

U.S. Units	Canadian Metric	Australian Metric
1/4 teaspoon	1 mL	1 ml
1/2 teaspoon	2 mL	2 ml
1 teaspoon	5 mL	5 ml
1 tablespoon	15 mL	20 ml
1/4 cup	50 mL	60 ml
1/3 cup	75 mL	80 ml
1/2 cup	125 mL	125 ml
2/3 cup	150 mL	170 ml
3/4 cup	175 mL	190 ml
1 cup	250 mL	250 ml
1 quart	1 liter	1 liter
1 1/2 quarts	1.5 liters	1.5 liters
2 quarts	2 liters	2 liters
2 1/2 quarts	2.5 liters	2.5 liters
3 quarts	3 liters	3 liters
4 quarts	4 liters	4 liters

WEIGHT

U.S. Units	Canadian Metric	Australian Metric
1 ounce	30 grams	30 grams
2 ounces	55 grams	60 grams
3 ounces	85 grams	90 grams
4 ounces (1/4 pound)	115 grams	125 grams
8 ounces (1/2 pound)	225 grams	225 grams
16 ounces (1 pound)	455 grams	500 grams
1 pound	455 grams	1/2 kilogram

Note: The recipes in this cookbook have not been developed or tested using metric measures. When converting recipes to metric, some variations in quality may be noted.

MEASUREMENTS

Inches	Centimeters
1	2.5
2	5.0
3	7.5
4	10.0
5	12.5
6	15.0
7	17.5
8	20.5
9	23.0
10	25.5
11	28.0
12	30.5
13	33.0
14	35.5
15	38.0

TEMPERATURES

Fahrenheit	Celsius
32°	0°
212°	100°
250°	120°
275°	140°
300°	150°
325°	160°
350°	180°
375°	190°
400°	200°
425°	220°
450°	230°
475°	240°
500°	260°

Index

Page numbers in *italics* indicate photographs.

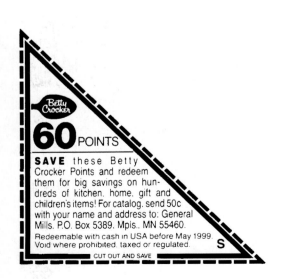